WHAT COMES AFTER DEATH?
The Reality of Heaven and Hell

BASILEA SCHLINK

What Comes after Death?

The Reality of Heaven and Hell

Creation House
Carol Stream, Illinois

United States edition published by Creation House,
499 Gundersen Drive, Carol Stream, Illinois 60187

Unless otherwise stated, all Bible quotations are taken from the
Revised Standard Version of the Bible, copyrighted 1946 and
1952 by the Division of Christian Education of the National
Council of the Churches of Christ in the U.S.A., and used
by permission.

Further quotations taken from
The Living Bible © 1971 Tyndale House Publishers,
paraphrased by Kenneth Taylor, published by
Coverdale House Publishers and used by permission.

The Amplified Bible, Old Testament,
Copyright © 1962, 1964 Zondervan Publishing House,
used by permission.

Quotations from St. Teresa are from *The Complete Works of
St. Teresa,* translated and edited by E. Allison Peers, published
by Sheed & Ward, London (American edition *The Life of Teresa
of Jesus - The Autobiography of St. Teresa of Avila,*
copyright © Sheed & Ward Inc., Kansas City, Missouri), and
are used by permission.

ISBN 0-88419-021-8
Library of Congress Catalog Card No. 76-51104
Printed in the United States of America

Contents

HEAVEN AND THE CITY OF GOD - THE PILGRIM'S
  GOAL!

DEATH AND THE KINGDOM OF HELL – THE DIE IS CAST IN THIS LIFE

Living in the Age of Death

The question of death is highly pertinent in our generation. Ultimately no one can evade the issue, even if most men repress the thought of death and avoid speaking about it, reluctant to face up to its reality and all its consequences. But it is an irrefutable fact that the prince of death has a tighter grip upon the earth, upon mankind, than ever before in the history of the world. He has stepped into power and seems to have command over everything.

This was prophesied in the Word of God. In Revelation 6 we read that the pale horse will appear at the end of time and that its rider, whose name is Death, will be given power. In other words, at a specific period of time Death will be granted a specific amount of authority by God. He will be given power to kill a fourth of mankind (Revelation 6:8). In our age this is not only within the realm of possibility, but leading nuclear physicists have predicted that this would be the result of a nuclear war.

Yet even now, before the outbreak of a nuclear war, Death has started to establish his dominion. A large-scale dying has begun. Death's precursor is, so to speak, sweeping through the world today and heralding the approach of the rider on the pale horse.

The death of fish and birds has assumed alarming proportions owing to air and water pollution, and throughout the world plant life is dying.[1] Scientists say that if animals can no longer live because of a polluted environment, man will not be able to live much longer either. Today the pollution of air, soil and water and the contamination of foodstuffs are rapidly increasing. The number of sick cases and deaths due to pollution is rising. A friend in France, for instance, wrote

[1] See Basilea Schlink, *Pollution: but there* is *an answer* (British edition) or *A Matter of Life and Death* (American edition).

to us, saying, 'I was critically ill for a year. It was a new disease, caused by the chemical pollution of the air. I was like one of the burnt victims of Hiroshima, and for months my life hung in the balance. . . .'

In addition to the growing number of new and mysterious diseases resulting from pollution, cancer is said to be the cause of almost one out of every five deaths in West Germany today. But these are not the only means by which Death is gradually extending his rule throughout the world. How frequent are news items in the daily press such as: 'Charter plane turns into a mass grave' – 'Aeroplane crashes in flames, over 120 dead' – '129 traffic deaths on Easter weekend in West Germany' – 'Total of 64 killed in 3 bus accidents' – '50 killed in jet crash' – 'Department store fire with 13 dead'! And so we could continue. There are almost 19,000 deaths on the road every year in West Germany, and there are annually 250,000 deaths on the streets of the world.

The seal of death has been imprinted upon the whole earth. Death lurks in the air; it lurks on the streets; and it lurks in foodstuffs. Death even uses our fellow men as his instruments, as we can see from the soaring crime rate and the growing lawlessness. Nowadays no one can be sure that he will not suddenly be kidnapped and held hostage. In the year 1971, 16,000 people were murdered in the United States. And from year to year the number of murders rises at an alarming rate. On the basis of factual reports and statistics a specialist in the German criminal investigation department has deduced that by 1980 there will be 11 murders committed per day in West Germany. Throughout the world unborn children are being killed by the million. In addition, there are many millions in atheistic countries who are being put to death because of their faith in God or their refusal to submit to a dictatorship. About 25 million people in the world die of starvation every year. With the growing frequency of droughts and floods and other severe natural catastrophes, Death is claiming many more victims.

It is a fact – we are living in the age of death! Death, whom our fathers often portrayed as a skeleton with a scythe, is using drugs to reap a rich harvest among the youth, the flower of the nations. Heroin is a common cause of death in our day. Gloating triumphantly, Death watches while young people take drugs and keep increasing the dosage until he finally mows them down and they taste death as the wages of sin. And often enough it is the young people who fall into his clutches by committing suicide, which, next to traffic accidents, is the second most common cause of death among young people in the United States. In West Germany 13,000 people committed suicide in 1973 and the figures are rising. In addition, diseases that were partly due to smoking took the large toll of 140,000 deaths in West Germany, in 1972.

Death has begun to celebrate his heyday. His power will wax daily until death will be virtually the only thing we read of, hear of and see: murder, abortion, suicide, fatal traffic casualties, death caused by air pollution, poisoning and drugs as well as an increasing number of new fatal diseases. The precursor of the rider on the pale horse already seems to be exerting great influence over the world – and when a nuclear war breaks out, Death will reap an immense harvest. Therefore, it is inexcusable if those of us who believe in Jesus do not confront the issue of death.

What is Death?

Death is terrible and frightening! Even people who mocked at Death grew frightened when he drew near them. It was not without reason that the old masters portrayed Death as a formidable figure evoking horror and dread. This is how God must have shown Death to them, for God-fearing painters, it is said, saw in spirit many of the scenes that they portrayed in their works – the heavenly world with the angels as well as the judgment of God and the realm of hell. And we too sense that Death is a gruesome figure to be feared.

Ice-cold is Death; in his presence all warm, pulsating life dies. He can turn a living man into a corpse. Even the most vivacious life he renders motionless, causing all signs of life to cease. A dead person is no longer aware of human voces. He no longer hears the singing of birds or the howling of the wind. He is unaware of sunshine and rain, heat and cold, love and hatred. A dead man can no longer express himself; he does not show any reactions.

Moreover, Death is relentless and gruesome. He snatches people away from those who love and need them. He wipes out entire nations and races. Exulting in his power and full of scorn, he extinguishes flourishing lives and lays them in the grave, where all that remains to be said is, 'Earth to earth, ashes to ashes, dust to dust.'

The Bible records not only that Jesus wept at Lazarus' tomb, but that He was 'moved with indignation', yes, even 'moved with deep anger' – presumably at the power of Death (John 11:33, 38 *The Living Bible*). Man, when he is alive, is full of life and spirit, but when he dies, his flesh will be eaten by worms in the grave. Wherever Death puts in his sickle, decay follows, and no one can prevent this, for the power of Death is very great.

Most likely Death is a satanic prince, for as it is written

n Hebrews 2:14, the devil 'has the power of death'. Perhaps Death is the mightiest prince of darkness, for in Holy Scripture he is called the last enemy to be destroyed (1 Corinthians 15:26). It is clear from the statements of Scripture that Death is a person and not merely a force, a condition or a place – and by no means a 'nothing'. It is written: 'Death and Hades gave up the dead in them . . . Then Death and Hades were thrown into the lake of fire' (Revelation 20:13f); 'I have the keys of Death and Hades' (Revelation 1:18). The vision of John in Revelation 6:8 indicates even more clearly that Death is a person. There we read that the rider on the pale horse is called 'Death' and that 'Hades [the realm of the dead] followed him'. Thus Death is the lord of Hades and the dead are his retinue. Accordingly, in Revelation Death and Hades are always named together as two distinct entities, and this would be meaningless if they were identical.

In Gethsemane Jesus wrestled with Death. He suffered severe agony as He confronted that gruesome enemy, the prince of death. During this battle Jesus' sweat fell to the ground like great drops of blood. And it was probably when Jesus, the pure and sinless Son of God, full of light, saw this evil, satanic figure closing in on Him that He began to be filled with 'horror and deepest distress' (Mark 14:33 *The Living Bible*).

Death is also referred to as a power. The psalmists, for instance, when describing horrifying experiences, write: 'The cords of death encompassed me . . . the snares of death confronted me'; 'Thou dost lay me in the dust of death' (Psalm 18:4f; 22:15).

Death is indeed a power to which everyone must submit. For every single person a day has been appointed when Death will come to him. No one can escape Death. Even the mightiest man on earth must yield to him. Death is a tyrant whom millions and millions must obey. He exercises his power in all spheres of life. Everything and everyone must obediently submit to him. Kings and despots are overcome by him; and the most gruesome dictators cannot flee from him.

But there is more to the issue of death. For Death not only mows us down, robs us of the breath of life and prevents us from doing or accomplishing anything more on earth. It will not be 'all over' then, as many assume who hope to evade the problems of this life by seeking their refuge in death, which they regard as a 'nothing'. Nor according to the testimony of the Bible is death a state of sleep that awaits the deceased, even if some Bible passages do use this word (cf. 1 Corinthians 15:20; 1 Thessalonians 4:13). These passages do not make an absolute statement about the condition of the dead; the word 'sleep' is probably used only to describe the outward appearance of the dead. Other Bible verses, for instance the passages in Revelation mentioned earlier, clearly indicate that the dead – if they have not experienced the redeeming power of Jesus – will be led by the prince of death into his kingdom. True, not until the Last Judgment will God pronounce His final verdict, 'Depart from me, you cursed, into the eternal fire' (Matthew 25:41), but even so the intermediate condition of the unsaved dead is a 'place of torment' as it is written in the story of the rich man in Luke 16:28.

Death lays a rightful claim to the people whom he takes into his kingdom, for 'the wages of sin is death' (Romans 6:23). As sinners we belong to him. Sin, in other words, makes us a prey of Death and the powers of darkness in Satan's realm of death. These are established facts. Here on earth we can see in a small way how our sins bring death. Carnal sins ruin our bodies and our strength. Sins of the soul, such as hatred and envy, destroy our inner peace, our vitality and our relationship with others. Sin destroys our security in God, our eternal hope and our love for God and our neighbour. How dreadful, then, must be the effects wrought by the power of Death in his kingdom, where all façades will be removed.

Jesus, the Vanquisher of Death

When we consider the reality of Death in all his gruesomeness, we can scarcely comprehend that someone came to enter combat with Death. Yet Someone did come – Jesus Christ! He destroyed the power of Death. This is a fact. Jesus – and He alone – gave Himself into the power of Death in order to take away his sting. The power of the mighty prince of death was broken when it came up against the almighty Lord. But how did Jesus vanquish Death? It was not by uttering a word of authority. Sin had to be blotted out, because it is our sin that gives the prince of death power over us. Yet it surpasses all human comprehension that Jesus gave Himself to suffer in our stead the wrath and judgment of God that our sin has incurred – indeed, He even suffered death. For our sakes Jesus endured the untold torment that would otherwise have awaited us in the kingdom of the dead.

It is understandable that Death fell upon Jesus with all his might, for through Jesus' suffering and death upon the cross Death was deprived of his right to the souls of men, whom he would otherwise have taken into his kingdom of torment upon their decease. Thus Death vented his fury on Jesus, making Him taste hell and suffer all the horrors, terrors and methods of torture that he had reserved for the souls who belong to him because of their sin. Never shall we be able to picture how gruesome Jesus' battle in Gethsemane actually was. Jesus may well have been tormented by all the methods of physical, emotional and mental torture that the kingdom of the dead and hell inflict upon their subjects according to their sins. All this He endured as a lamb, wholly submitted to the will of God in immeasurable love for us, in order to redeem us. Indeed, He became obedient unto death, even death on a cross.

2

Where has such love ever been found? The eternal, sinless and thus immortal Lord tasted death, the wages of sin, for the sake of us men, who so often hate Him, today as long ago, loving darkness instead. Who can comprehend such amazing love of God? 'A Lamb goes uncomplaining forth, the guilt of all men bearing'; He bleeds to death, so that Death can no longer exert his power over us for ever, having vented all his fury on Jesus. Now we can sing, 'Death, where are thy terrors now?' and pray in adoration, 'Praise be to Him who has overcome Death!' In triumphant joy we may proclaim, 'Death, where is thy victory? . . . Death, where is thy sting? . . . But thanks be to God, who gives us the victory through our Lord Jesus Christ' (1 Corinthians 15:55, 57).

Jesus is the mighty Victor over Death as He proved immediately after He accomplished His act of redemption at Calvary, for the Holy Scriptures record how in saving love He hastened to those who were languishing in the prison of death. In the first letter of Peter it is written that in the spirit He 'went and preached to the spirits in prison, who formerly did not obey, when God's patience waited in the days of Noah, during the building of the ark, in which a few, that is, eight persons, were saved through water' (1 Peter 3:19f).

But who will experience that Jesus is Victor over Death? Only those who truly believe in Jesus, the risen Lord, as their Redeemer, because they have been born again by the Spirit of God. Indeed, only those who reckon ever anew with the victory of Jesus over all the powers of sin and death during their lifetime will experience in their last hour that Jesus is the Vanquisher of Death. These are people who refuse to tolerate any spiritual death in themselves. In the battle of faith they use the weapon of the victorious name of Jesus, and as humbled but pardoned sinners they look to their mighty Redeemer and Prince of life for everything.

However, even if faith in Jesus is the way to overcome the powers of Death, this does not necessarily imply that such believers will be spared the throes of death. It is imperative that we prepare ourselves for this last onslaught of the prince of death. This is the message of many songs written by believers who overcame their fear of death by looking to Jesus in faith. When death draws near, we are confronted with our sins and thus with the kingdom of hell and Satan, the accuser, who would normally have a right to us. Martin Luther wrote in a hymn:

> While in the midst of death we be,
>   Hell's grim powers o'ertake us.
> Who from such distress will free?
>   Who secure will make us?
> Thou only, Lord, canst do it! . . .
>
>   Let us not, we pray,
>   From the true faith's comfort
> Fall in our last need away.[1]

And to cite other hymn writers:

> When I am in the throes of death
> And I must draw my final breath,
> Lord Jesus, hasten to my side
>   And help me past the stormy tide . . .
>   Shorten death's agony.[2]
>
> Who knows how near my life's expended?
>   Time flies, and death is hasting on . . .
>   My God, for Jesus' sake, I pray
>   Thy peace may bless my dying day.[3]
>
> Shorten the pangs of death for me,
> And draw me home to dwell with Thee.[4]

[1] cf. *Evangelisches Kirchengesangbuch* (EKG) 309.
[2] Paul Eber, cf. EKG 314.
[3] Countess von Schwarzburg-Rudolstadt, cf. EKG 331.
[4] Benjamin Schmolck, cf. *Altes Bayrisches Gesangbuch* 543.

Help me, O Vanquisher of Death,
  Free me from fear and dread.
Thou wrestled with the powers of death
  That sinners might be saved.
And when at last the end draws near
  And Death lays hold on me,
Receive me, Lord, into Thy hands,
  For Thou hast ransomed me.[1]

Paul Gerhardt sang the verse:

Draw near me when I'm dying.
  O Saviour, take my part.
When fear would overwhelm me
  And terror fill my heart
By Thine own fear and suff'ring
  Make all my fears depart.[2]

Thus it is vital that everyone, including those who believe in Jesus Christ as their Saviour, fully confront the reality of death – especially today when everyone is threatened with death more than ever before.

[1] Gottfried Benedict Funk, cf. *Altes Bayrisches Gesangbuch* 545.
[2] cf. EKG 63.

To be a Realist

'Teach us to number our days, that we may apply our hearts unto wisdom' (Psalm 90:12 AV). Today as never before, this must be our fervent plea. Let us be ever mindful that death is waiting for us and let us consider its consequences. None of us knows what the future holds. We do not know what the next few days, weeks, months and years will bring us. But one thing we know most assuredly – one day will be our last. One day we too shall meet our death – and perhaps very suddenly in this age when death is menacing us on all sides.

'The years of our life . . . are soon gone,' says Scripture even in reference to a normal life (Psalm 90:10). Our life is short and it only comes once. Indeed, it can be compared to a night's sleep – it passes by so swiftly. Or, as it says further on in Psalm 90, 'We are like grass that is green in the morning but mowed down and withered before the evening shadows fall' (verse 6 *The Living Bible*).

A wise man once said that our life on earth is like the flight of a bird through a large room – in one side and out the other, the bird's element being the air outside. Thus our life too is like the brief moments it takes to cross a room. But our element is elsewhere. Our real home is not here on earth but in the next world, where we shall live for ever. The span of our earthly life is so short that it does not even make up a fraction of the time that we shall spend in the next world. For what are seventy or eighty years – assuming that we are granted such a long life – compared with our life in eternity, which has no end? Whoever is wise, therefore, will consider his death.

Our death and thus eternity is a reality - indeed, far more of a reality than this earth, for the world in its present form will pass away. But eternity is a realm where nothing will pass away, where everything remains for ever. It is a fact that here on earth all created things are bound to come to an end in one way or another. Even man, the crown of creation, must return to dust and ashes after a certain period of time. 'When thou takest away their breath, they die and return to their dust' (Psalm 104:29). All that we have worked for, all that we have created can be eaten away by moths and rust. It will disintegrate with wear and tear, and with the ravages of time, as is the fate of all earthly things, or be destroyed by natural catastrophes and wars. And one day the earth itself will explode with a terrific tearing blast and the elements will be dissolved with fire (cf. 2 Peter 3:10–12). With the invention of nuclear weapons such an event is not difficult to imagine, even if it is actually the hand of God executing judgment.

If this transient earth is not our real home, but merely an intermediate station, where will our home be for the whole span of eternity? Many of our forefathers confronted this reality clearly and lived ever mindful of death. Merchants in earlier centuries would write in large letters on the first page of their accounting books, '*Memento mori*' – 'think of death', that is, think of your last hour.

Whoever is a realist will think of his death and eternity. For eternity is a permanent state, which we shall enter perhaps very soon – at the latest in a few decades. The typical trait of a realist is that he makes provisions in advance. But it is shortsighted to make provisions only for the brief years of one's old age. Do we make provisions for the years that will follow in the next world, where we shall abide for ever? Do we make provisions for a happy life there? Is the question, 'Where shall I spend eternity?' of vital importance to us?

Let us bear in mind that during the very brief period of our earthly lives we can either gain or forfeit everything in the way of glory for all eternity. This is a weighty matter. If we know that here on earth we could miss out on a large inheritance and thus great opportunities for our life due to a small mistake, an act of carelessness, or lack of diligence on our part, we would consider the matter vastly important. But have we considered what we could lose and forfeit for all eternity? Have we clearly confronted what awaits us after death in one kingdom or the other depending on what we have done in our earthly body, whether it was good or evil (2 Corinthians 5:10)?

To take an illustration from our earthly life, we have a rough idea of what would await us if we were sent to a concentration camp, and we would accordingly do everything possible to escape such a fate. Yet a sentence spent in such a gruesome place would last only for a limited amount of time, for everyone who is not released will be taken by death at the hour appointed by God. But there will be no end to the torment in the places of terror in the kingdom of hell. It will be a judgment of fire in eternity. Therefore, in the face of death and eternity, we are being challenged by the Lord to consider what is at stake. Whoever does not count the cost will one day have to suffer the bitter consequences of his foolishness in a place of torment, void of peace, light, comfort and hope.

The All-revealing Hour of Death

Death brings with it the exposure of our entire life – for believers and non-believers alike. All the façades that we so often use to deceive ourselves and others during our earthly existence collapse before the holiness of God. The most shattering examples of this unmasking can be seen in the lives of great God-haters and those who denied His existence, for in the hour of death many people are confronted with truths that they had sought to gainsay all their lives. During his lifetime the French philosopher Voltaire proclaimed that there is no God and no such thing as eternity or judgment – this he declared to be the truth. But we are told that when his end drew near he was filled with terror at the gruesome reality of death, which stood relentlessly before him. There was no escape. At the same time he had to confront the reality of sin. With that the last delusion and assertion, yes, every last dream of an autonomous man disappeared for Voltaire, who with his keen intellect and arguments had propagated the theory of an autonomous man who has no need to recognize a God or Lord over him. He had raised his head against this God and Lord, mocked and blasphemed Him, and now he had to face the truth – but at this stage the truth spelt only judgment for him.

Death is ordained by God to teach us the truth – namely, the truth that we are a mere nothing and shall return to dust and ashes. But this is not all. Death opens even the blindest of eyes to see that man is the work of God's hands, created in His image, an ethical being with a sense of responsibility and therefore required to give account of himself at the end of his life. As portrayed in the Gospel of John, Jesus has come into the world 'to bear witness to the truth', so that we may 'know the truth' while there is still time. He promises us, 'The truth will make you free', for He is 'the way, and the truth, and the life'. But because He proclaimed the truth, men sought to kill Him. Not until we are in heaven, shall we fully realize what great pains Jesus took to shed the light of divine truth into our darkened lives. He longs that we might learn to 'love the truth' (2 Thessalonians 2:10) and be more and more pervaded by light so as to be made fit for His kingdom.

But in contrast to Jesus, Satan tries to keep us under a delusion all our lives. He takes care that we lie to ourselves and want to be lied to. Therefore he rejoices when the impenitent do not see the fatal truth until their dying hour when it is conveyed to them by the prince of death – the truth about their sin, their guilt-laden life. By then it is often too late for a person to repent and turn from his former ways; it is only seldom that a genuine about-turn can be made in the hour of death.

As Death approached Voltaire with this truth about sin and judgment, he fell into despair. He accused his friends of having brought him into such a state and cursed them. In the presence of two witnesses he even drew up a document in which he renounced his disbelief, but this formality did not indicate a genuine change of heart. His doctor found him in great fear. 'I am forsaken by God and man!' Voltaire cried out. He then offered the doctor half his fortune if he could extend his life for six months. But it was too late. When the doctor told him that he did not even have six weeks to live, Voltaire cried out, 'Then I shall go to hell and you will go with me!' [1]

How terrifying Death is! Who, therefore, knowing the Victor over Death and believing in Him as his personal Saviour, would not beseech Him, 'My God, for Jesus' sake, I pray Thy peace may bless my dying day.' For it is a shattering reality that the other world draws near in the hour of death. Either angels enter the room of the dying person and

[1] cf. Fr. Rienecker, *Das Schönste kommt noch* (Wuppertal, 1965), Vol. I, p. 87.

the presence of God is so real that we do not dare raise our voices; or else evil spirits draw close, filling us with horror and dread. Gloating triumphantly, they can scarcely wait until they can claim those who led a life of sin and served Satan, taking them as their prey into the realm of torment in order to apply their methods of torture.

The presence of the powers of darkness could also be felt at Stalin's death. His daughter Svetlana wrote: 'My father died a difficult and terrible death . . . the death agony was horrible. He literally choked to death as we watched. At what seemed like the very last moment he suddenly opened his eyes . . . it was a terrible glance, insane or perhaps angry and full of the fear of death . . . then he suddenly lifted his left hand as though he were pointing to something above and bringing down a curse on us all. The gesture was incomprehensible and full of menace. . . .'[1]

The spirits of the other world, angels or demons, will come for us in the hour of our death. This we can see from the story of the poor man Lazarus, whom the angels carried to Abraham's bosom, to paradise (Luke 16:22). That our dwelling-place in the next world is already decided to some extent in the hour of our death and not only later at the Last Judgment is also evident from Jesus' words to the good thief on the cross, 'Today you will be with me in Paradise' (Luke 23:43).

[1] Svetlana Alliluyeva, *Twenty Letters to a Friend* (Hutchinson, London; Harper & Row, New York, 1967).

A Dangerous Delusion

Who will come for us in the hour of our death? A parish worker once related how she had served for many years in a church that had a reputation for being especially 'religious' – the members were born-again believers. Yet at the deathbeds of some of these church members she was deeply distressed to see old people, believing Christians, die a terrible death. Indeed, the power of darkness could be sensed in the rooms of the dying. Later this woman was transferred to another church where the members were God-fearing in the truest sense of the word. And she noticed that the sick there usually had a much easier death. What could be the explanation? Jesus says, 'Not every one who says to me, "Lord, Lord," shall enter the kingdom of heaven, but he who does the will of my Father who is in heaven' (Matthew 7:21). Thus in the second church the members may have had less knowledge of God, but what little they knew they put into practice with God-fearing hearts. In the especially 'religious' church, on the other hand, the people may have known much, but done little – the great danger for us believers at all times. This is how Satan gains such power!

Those who are convinced that the angels of God will carry them into the kingdom of glory in the hour of death will have a terrible shock if instead they have to hear and experience Jesus' verdict one day that the first are now the last and vice versa. God revealed this truth most vividly to one of the fathers of Pietism, Jung-Stilling. In his well-known book about scenes from the realm of spirits, *Szenen aus dem Geisterreiche*,[1] Jung-Stilling depicts a few figures wandering about confusedly in the realm of shadows, lonely and unhappy. Significantly enough, all of them had been believers, contemporaries of Jung-Stilling.

[1] Elberfeld, 1933. The following is a résumé of the eighth scene.

One of them complains, 'I am at a loss as to what to say. It was our firm conviction that we would be given precedence in going to heaven. But can you imagine, brother, I saw that many of those whom we did not think were born-again have been led by the angels in triumph into the kingdom of the blessed. But so far no angel has taken any notice of me.'

Of another soul wandering about sad and forlorn in this realm of shadows, it is said, 'A short while ago he approached one of the heavenly messengers, but the poor soul was hurled far away by the electric shock that proceeded from the angel like a bolt of lightning.'

The souls are utterly bewildered at all this, for they had held this particular man in high esteem. 'His gift of eloquence and knowledge was so great that we acknowledged him as our leader. His exemplary life in the presence of God, his detachment from the world and his faithfulness in pointing out what was amiss in our lives convinced us all that he would receive a glorious inheritance here!' Instead this soul and all the others drift about in the realm of shadows in darkness, looking wretched and emaciated. No angel deems them worthy of a glance, for there is no trace of Jesus' image to be seen in them.

One of them says, 'If deception is still possible here, then the Word of God is not the Word of God! No, I believe that the souls whom we saw being taken away were being conveyed to places of purification. Perhaps it is evil spirits who have come for them in the guise of angels of light!'

The second replies, 'That's not the way it seems to me!' But their conversation does not lead them to any conclusion.

Then a third calls out, 'What do I see there? What glorious beings are these descending the mountains in the light of the rising sun?'

'They are angels who judge the souls [by this a preliminary judgment is meant]. Would you like a look?'

'Do you see Brother E. standing before the angel? O Lord,

he's shrinking into a dwarf! Now a flame is shooting out of him! Do you see the terrible things in the red flame?'

'It is awful! Almighty, merciful God! He's changing into a monster. . . .' [His appearance now reflects his true self and being, which was so evil.]

The souls in the realm of shadows continue their conversation. 'See how he flies away into the night with a hissing sound, as though the flame were singeing him!'

The deceased now see another angel standing before a soul, who begins to glow with an aura of ever-increasing light. One of the deceased says, 'I know him. Is that not the schoolmaster Elias? He was very ill when I died. But surely that cannot be him. This soul is so transfigured, he looks like a saint. But the schoolmaster was not even born-again!'

An angel draws close to them. 'Yes, this indeed was the schoolmaster Elias. Now he is a prince in the land of the righteous and his inheritance is magnificent.'

The first soul addresses the angel, saying, 'Excuse me, O glorious one, if I may be so bold as to ask you a question. We cannot understand how this schoolmaster can go to heaven, when he was not even born-again. Don't the angels know what "born-again" means?'

The angel replied, 'Whether we know it or not is not the question – rather whether you know it.'

The believer answered, 'Praise God! I know it, for I have been born-again for over forty years. A person is born again when he recognizes his sinful wretchedness and repents wholeheartedly of his extremely corrupt state, turning to God and Christ in all sincerity.'

Now comes the most crucial point in the angel's reply: 'The concept in itself is perfectly right and the commandment it contains is a welcome duty to those who wish to go to heaven. But you sought to fulfil your religious duties solely with pious devotions, Bible reading, praying and hymn-singing. To be sure, you avoided the more obvious sins, but you harboured and fostered the more subtle ones, which are far worse – spiritual pride, feigned humility, disdain and criticism of those who were better than you. And not only have you done so, but you have considered it to be zeal for the House of God. You have always taken pains to know what to do in order to please God, but you have taken this knowledge for action.'

Do we too take our knowledge for action?

The angel went on to say, 'All mortification and crucifixion [of self] without true and active love is an abomination to God, for it only fosters pride. Who goes to further lengths in the mortification of all desires of the flesh than the fakirs in India? But who is more proud? As long as you have not cut off this source of pride and faultfinding in yourself, you cannot go to heaven.'

Thereupon came the answer of the souls in the realm of shadows, revealing their deep-seated pride. 'But in our soul we had the deep assurance of being children of God and the Spirit bore witness to us of this!'

'The true witness of being a child of God,' rejoined the angel, 'is expressed in heartfelt humility. Remember how good the Pharisee felt in his heart when he could say, "God, I thank Thee that I am not like other men, that I am not a sinner like this tax collector." But how can this confidence [this superior attitude and spirit of criticism] be a witness of being a child of God? You have all been exposed before the judgment seat of the Sovereign of the world; your innermost heart has been laid bare and you can see your whole life lying before you with the utmost clarity and yet in your pride you aim higher still, laying claim to the Kingdom of God. Beware that you do not fall under the judgment of the rebels!'

But even at this admonition these believers had only a pious answer. Then the angel began to shine most frighteningly. 'Depart with haste, so that the wrathful fire of the Most High does not cast you into the outermost darkness! You think that your love is stronger than hell, but you have not even begun to love. Begone!'

Behind this scene depicted by Jung-Stilling are biblical truths. Jesus loves us and has paid a high price for our redemption. How much then must He yearn to take us into His kingdom as the fruit of His suffering and receive us there with the words, 'Come, O blessed of my Father. Enter into the joy of your master!' (Matthew 25:34, 21).

But what a grief it is for Jesus when, in spite of His precious sacrifice, souls that He has redeemed cannot enter His kingdom, even though they counted themselves among the believers! Much to Jesus' grief such believers did not take to heart the words, 'Depart!' and 'I do not know you', which He spoke time and again as a warning for those who were so sure that they belonged to Him. They took their knowledge for action, as the angel said. They were so confident that the gates of the Kingdom of God would be open for them and that they would be present at the Marriage Feast of the Lamb.

Let us remember the parable of the ten virgins – 'five of them were foolish'. The foolish virgins never imagined it possible that the door could be closed to them one day, for had they not gone out to meet the Bridegroom? Thus we could liken them to devout people who read the Bible, pray and are active in evangelistic outreach. 'On that day many will say to me, "Lord, Lord, did we not prophesy in your name, and cast out demons in your name, and do many mighty works in your name?" And then will I declare to them, "I never knew you; depart from me, you evildoers"' (Matthew 7:22f). They incur such a severe verdict, since they had forgotten to do the simplest things that are expected of a disciple of Jesus, that is, of a believer: they had failed to do His will and obey His commandments not to criticize, quarrel, be angry or irreconciled, embittered, proud or condemning.

It was on account of these very sins that Jesus' wrath came upon the religious people of His day, the Pharisees. They clung to their sins, they continued to transgress without any qualms and refused to recognize Him as the Saviour, who had come to save and deliver those who grieve over their sins. Although it is an irrefutable fact that, as the Victor over Death, Jesus has delivered us from Death and the kingdom of the dead, we must claim this redemption and let it be manifest in our lives. Otherwise the hour of death will disclose that we did not truly believe in Jesus.

A true and living faith in Jesus Christ keeps us in constant touch with Him, the living Lord. The person that truly believes is convicted by the Holy Spirit of the sins he commits day by day – an experience that brings him to contrition and repentance. This in turn will drive him ever anew to Jesus, for as a sinful being who continually heaps fresh guilt upon himself he has to claim Jesus' redemption daily. This kind of faith bears the opposite characteristic to the faith of the proud, faultfinding believers in Jung-Stilling's book. Humility is its salient feature, a broken and contrite heart that does not criticize and condemn others or become aloof with a feeling of superiority, but rather seeks to be reconciled in humble love.

Soon the hour will come when Death will stand at our deathbed, when he will unmask and accuse us. Like all other princes of darkness he is probably granted the right to accuse souls; for as it is written in Revelation 12:10, Satan can even come before God to accuse men. Whenever he has an opportunity to accuse a soul, he laughs scornfully and exults with his demons, while Jesus and His angels mourn. But there is joy in heaven when a soul repents – even if it be at the very last moment as with the thief on the cross. Then the soul will experience that Jesus is the Victor over Death and has deprived the accuser of his power.

God Warns, Because He is Love

God makes every effort to forewarn us, so that Death will not appear as the accuser in the hour of our death and Satan will not be able to send his servants to conduct us to the kingdom of the dead. The Lord warns us in His Word, He lets us hear sermons, He gives us books to read and sends people into our lives. In order to shake us out of our complacency, He brings us now and then into situations where our lives are threatened: severe illnesses, critical operations, traffic accidents, the perils of war and other dangers. In this way we are taught to confront Death, our accuser and the exposer of our sins, so that we may turn from our former ways and repent while there is still time. God uses every possible means to confront us with our sins, so that we can bring them to Jesus, our Redeemer. He wants to shake us out of our complacency towards sin, so that we shall earnestly fight the battle of faith against sin every day and submit to His chastening in order to partake of His holiness.

Consequently, these divine interventions are often bound up with a powerful, instantaneous realization of guilt. People saved from drowning have related that during what seemed to be their last moments scenes from their lives suddenly flashed through their minds like a film reel being played back and they were deeply shocked to be shown sins that they had never realized before.

A parallel can be drawn to the time when Martin Luther narrowly escaped being killed by a stroke of lightning. A sudden realization of his guilt made him cry out, 'What shall I do for God to be gracious to me?' This is an example of God's untiring work of love to warn us. Down through the ages God in His love has sought to save man by warnings.

This we also experienced in the lives of the young people who attended our girls' Bible study groups, which later

3

developed into our Sisterhood. During the Hitler era they professed Jesus Christ and gathered every week round the Bible. The young people knew and acknowledged that Jesus is the Saviour, who frees man from sin and guilt. This was part of their faith, just as it was for the believers in Jung-Stilling's narrative. But it was no more than that. They did not grieve over the specific sins that marred their personalities and everyday lives. Contrition was a purely theoretical matter to them – equally so were breaking with sin, turning from their former ways, rejoicing over the redemption Jesus' blood had wrought and love for Jesus. But then Death drew near to them. In September 1944 our city, Darmstadt, was hit by an air raid. A terrible hail of bombs descended upon us, laying almost the entire city in ruins within eighteen minutes. Thousands lost their lives. Many were burnt to death in the air-raid shelters or in their attempt to escape through the burning streets. During those critical minutes our young people sat in their air-raid shelters in fear of death. Death stood before them. Would they now fall prey to him? They were gripped by deep horror. Death had come to accuse them and unmask their lives. Suddenly they were confronted with sins that they had committed against God and man – there was no escaping the issue. Sin had become a reality for them, an object of horror that made them cry out to Jesus and beg forgiveness and deliverance.

The Hitler regime had brought many hardships upon Christians, including our young people. And what this suffering failed to accomplish now occurred as a result of the air raid when Death drew near. Sinners were unmasked. Eternity became a terrifying reality. Many of our young people heard the verdict of God in their hearts, 'Not prepared for death, not prepared for eternity!' – for up till then they had not been living mindful of death and eternity. 'Because you are lukewarm . . . I will spew you out of my mouth' (Revelation 3:16). These words of Jesus seemed like a death sentence to them. Their Christian lives were characterized by lukewarmness. There was no battle against sin, no hatred of sin, no ardent love for Jesus constraining them to sacrifice, suffer and lose their lives for Him, no love for souls, no burning desire to save them, no fervency of prayer. What would have been their fate if they had been snatched away by Death in that hour? Jesus would have cast them out of His presence – they would have been spewed out of His mouth.

God spared the lives of most of them, brought them to contrition and repentance and inspired them with love for Jesus. They now began a new life with Him, a life lived for Him. Using the air raid as a warning, God taught them to see the reality of eternity.

But all of us who are living in the age of death today have been forewarned and are being warned ever anew. Before God the Father is forced to pour out His terrible wrath and make cities, forests, meadows and even whole countries disappear from the face of the earth, He is now sending preliminary judgments to all parts of the earth. One region after another, one country after another is being hit by flood disasters, drought, tornadoes, volcanic eruptions, epidemics, emergency situations due to pollution, forest fires, severe storms and famine. But also events such as strikes, acts of terror and violent revolutions are preliminary judgments for us.[1]

As long as God continues to extend the time of grace, Jesus seeks to bring us to repentance. In His boundless love He woos us, for He is our Saviour, and He yearns to save us from the power of Death. Thus He entreats us to come to Him with our sins, so that He can wash them away with His blood. Then Death, the accuser, will lose his claim on us.

[1] See Basilea Schlink, *Countdown to World Disaster – Hope and Protection for the Future.*

The Gate is Narrow

Who were the people – other than the disciples – that were with Jesus the most? The inhabitants of the city of Capernaum and the neighbouring towns of Chorazin and Bethsaida. Thousands of devout people lived in these cities; they followed Jesus in droves – and not only because they sought healing. They would lay all else aside in order to hear words of eternal life from Jesus' lips. And yet Jesus pronounced that terrible verdict over them: 'Woe to you, Chorazin! woe to you, Bethsaida! for if the mighty works done in you had been done in Tyre and Sidon, they would have repented long ago in sackcloth and ashes. But I tell you, it shall be more tolerable on the day of judgment for Tyre and Sidon than for you' (Matthew 11:21f).

And then Jesus went on to ask, 'And you, Capernaum, will you be exalted to heaven?' A justified question, for Capernaum was a chosen and favoured city. Its inhabitants heard Jesus more than other people and saw His mighty deeds, because He lived there. They paid Him homage and even wanted to make Him King, because they so loved and revered Him and enjoyed listening to His teaching. And now Jesus said of Capernaum and the people who dwelt there, 'You shall be brought down to Hades. For if the mighty works done in you had been done in Sodom, it would have remained until this day. But I tell you that it shall be more tolerable on the day of judgment for the land of Sodom than for you' (Matthew 11:23f).

Were not Sodom and Gomorrah the cities that were so steeped in immorality and wickedness that fire and brimstone rained down upon them? They were completely destroyed and all their inhabitants perished. And now Jesus was saying that these devout people of Capernaum, Bethsaida and Chorazin would fare worse on the day of judgment than Sodom and Gomorrah. Upon their decease the inhabitants of Capernaum would be led by the prince of death into the kingdom of the dead; they would not be able to enter the kingdom of Jesus – the kingdom of life, joy and peace, which Jesus had proclaimed in their midst and manifested in His person.

Why did Death have a right to these people when they so often came to listen to Jesus and brought others with them? How determined the people were to remain with Him in spite of their hunger and thirst, as we can see from the story of the feeding of the multitudes! How devout they were – so eager to hear Him! But they did not repent; they did not confess their sins and make a break with them. Therefore, despite their great receptiveness to Jesus' words, they remained under the influence of sin, Death and Hades.

With the hour of our death in mind let us heed the questions Jesus is asking us:

Did you repent each time you committed a sin?

If you said an unkind word, did you go to the one you hurt and say, 'Please forgive me'?

If you wronged or harmed someone, did you seek to make amends?

If you lied to someone, defrauded or robbed him, did you bring the matter into the light, confess it and put right what you did wrong?

If you yielded to the desires of the flesh in any way, did you turn round and walk in the opposite direction, taking the path of chastity and self-control?

If you had a false attachment to a person and gave him the love that belongs to the Lord, did you part company?

The first step towards a genuine act of repentance is shown to us in James 5:16, 'Confess your sins to one

35

another.' For 'if we confess our sins, he is faithful and just, and will forgive our sins and cleanse us from all unrighteousness' (1 John 1:9). If we always seek to avoid the humiliation of openly confessing our sins not only to God but before another person, our sin will remain unforgiven. It will retain its power over us and thus Death too will keep his hold over us. 'But when anything is exposed by the light it becomes visible, for anything that becomes visible is light' (Ephesians 5:13).

If we do not bring the sins that we have kept secret into the light, we shall one day have an experience similar to that of one dying man in China. A missionary related how this man, in the throes of death, suddenly cried out, 'Lost! Lost! It's too late! The gate is too narrow. I can't go in!' The Lord showed the missionary that an unconfessed sin was blocking the way for the man and preventing him from going to his eternal home as a saved soul. After the missionary spoke to him about this and the man confessed his sin, the anguish left him and he was immersed in peace. The dying man then said that he had seen in spirit the gate leading to glory, but was unable to squeeze through, because it was so narrow. It was his unconfessed sin that was preventing him from entering heaven and that was casting him into such despair. But now that he had confessed he could go to his eternal home with a transfigured expression on his face.[1]

Whoever is a realist and lives ever mindful of death will have the right attitude towards sin and take measures against it while there is still time. He will daily entreat God, 'Set my secret sins in the light of Thy countenance' (cf. Psalm 90:8). He will ask for light, because so often we are blind about our sins, especially as believers. We so easily grow self-confident and assume that everything is all right in our lives, since we 'live by grace' and 'grace is all-sufficient!'

[1] Elisabeth Seiler, *Berufen und geführt* (Telos-Bücher, Lahr-Dinglingen, 1971), pp. 93ff.

Whoever sincerely asks for light will also confess the sins he is shown.

Then if we are governed by sinful drives, for instance, or if any other sin seeks to keep us in its grip, we shall naturally follow Jesus' command and resolutely proceed against that sin. Better to lose a limb and overcome a sin than to persevere in it! The absolute demand of Jesus, 'Cut off your hand! Pluck out your eye!' can be understood only in the light of death and eternity, for according to Jesus' words sin that has not been overcome will have the terrible consequence that a person goes to hell (Matthew 5:29f). In contrast, 'he that overcometh shall inherit all things' (Revelation 21:7 AV). That is, only those who have fought the battle of faith against sin to the end will attain eternal salvation and joy. And what does this battle of faith entail? Just as the Israelites who had been bitten by serpents looked at the raised serpent, we must constantly look to Jesus, for we always need Him. In this way we shall be so closely knit to Jesus, our Saviour, that nothing will be able to separate us from Him.

Immortal, Divine Life

Whoever wants to have immortal life, so that Death cannot take him into his kingdom, must be connected to the source of life, Jesus. This immortal life, which is Jesus Himself, is like an eternal spring that never runs dry and that can never be overwhelmed by Death. Death cannot exert his power for ever over a person who bears this divine life, this life of Jesus, within himself.

How wonderful is God's offer of divine life! What a great deal it means to us in this age of death! Today more than ever it is vital that we possess this divine life. Death menaces us on all sides; demons rage about us. We do not know if we shall still be alive tomorrow. But if we have this eternal, divine life in us, we shall live, though we die. That is to say, this divine life will continue in the hour of our death, because it is immortal and cannot be killed. Death in all his gruesomeness has lost his power over us and has no right to take us into his kingdom of the dead.

The power contained in this divine life is evident, for instance, in aging people. When we grow old, all natural faculties steadily decrease: hearing, sight, mental abilities, memory, physical strength, etc. One could almost think that the aged are already under the power of Death, which will later be fully manifested in their dying hour. But Holy Scripture tells us otherwise. 'Though our outer nature is wasting away, our inner nature is being renewed every day' (2 Corinthians 4:16).

This I witnessed in my father's life. At the advanced age of ninety when all his mental and physical powers had diminished, one thing did not decrease and die, but rather increased all the more. This was Christ in him – the divine life, the joy that shone forth from him, the peace that ruled over him, the love that constrained him to pray for the

Kingdom of God and to bless others. Life, divine life flowed from him. Death could not touch this divine life that was in him, not even in the hour of death, which was filled with the radiance of eternity.

It is said of Johann Christoph Blumhardt[1] that in his old age he was stricken with the frailty that precedes death. Thus it often happened that he would fall asleep during family conversations. But this occurred only when they were discussing mundane affairs. As soon as the conversation turned to a spiritual topic and they began to speak of divine things, Blumhardt would instantly wake up and join in the conversation. Then he would pray powerfully and a stream of life would issue from his heart and lips. This too is an example of how life that comes from God is indestructible and victorious – also victorious over the precursors of death: weakness, fatigue, exhaustion and sleep.

How can we attain this divine life? When the rich young ruler asked this question, Jesus' reply was, 'Sell what you possess . . . and come, follow me' (Matthew 19:21). For him that would have meant parting with his wealth in exchange for eternal life, for entry into the Kingdom of God.

Each one of us is a 'rich young ruler' and in one way or another must part with his wealth and break with his idols. They occupy the place that Jesus wishes to occupy and that should be filled with eternal, divine life. For some it is money, for others it is their prestige, rights, people, goods, earthly desires. But faith in Jesus – which has the promise of eternal life (1 John 5:13) – and attachment to the things of this world are mutually exclusive. Jesus does not recognize a faith void of discipleship and obedience to His words, 'Give away! Relinquish! Take up your cross!'

[1] Johann Christoph Blumhardt (1805–80), a pastor in Möttlingen, Württemberg, who later became the leader of a Christian centre in Bad Boll. This spiritual counsellor was mightily used by God in bringing about a revival movement and was well known for his ministry of healing the sick and delivering the demon-possessed.

It is imperative that we take up Jesus' challenge today and 'sell all' so as to win the treasure of eternal, divine life, Jesus Himself, who is the Resurrection and the Life – for time is running out and Death is drawing close.

Divine life, nourished by faith and discipleship, will also be strengthened if we constantly feed upon the Word of God, love each other as He has bidden us, and have fellowship in the breaking of bread and in prayer as the Early Christians did (Acts 2:42). Should we not follow their example?

Death – the End of All Things

Many people tend to say, 'It's all over after death!' It is obvious that this is not true the way they mean it. But in a different sense this statement is very true and is especially significant for us as Christians. With the coming of death every opportunity to turn over a new leaf is gone. There are no more chances to work for God. An end is put to everything in our life. We can make no more amends.

Therefore, it is imperative that we confront this truth and start today at the very latest to live the way we shall wish to have lived on the day of our death. Now we must look to Jesus with eyes of faith and behold His sufferings and His sore wounds – the theme of many hymns – so that we can overcome in the hour of our death. Now before death approaches us, we must live in Jesus and have eternal, divine life in Him. This life cannot be killed by anything. Nor can it be 'washed out of us' by brain-washing. Though the outward man perish, the inward man increases all the more. Streams of living water will pour forth from such souls unto their dying hour and continue to flow even after death.

But death as 'the end of all things' is terrible for the soul who did not give Jesus room in his heart and in whom Jesus and His love did not dwell and divine life did not come to maturity because he 'loved darkness rather than light' (John 3:19). In the hour of death it is too late when we cry out in despair, 'Oh, if only I still had a chance to prove my love to the Lord Jesus or to one of my fellow men! If only I could bring Jesus a sacrifice! If only I could ask forgiveness of someone whom I have hurt or greatly wronged and make amends!' But in the throes of death this is no longer possible. Instead the terrible words 'too late' will resound over us. At that moment we would pay anything and make every effort to make up for that which we had failed to do.

When death strikes, the die is cast for our eternal dwelling-place. What it will be like depends upon the life that we have lived here on earth. Every single day we 'lay bricks' for eternity, whether we wish to realize it or not – either for the kingdom of the dead and hell or for heaven. In the story of the rich man and the beggar Lazarus, Jesus clearly shows us how significant is the path that we decide to follow during our lifetime. For the rich man it brought an irrevocable fate of torment, but for Lazarus a blessed destiny. Both experienced that whatever a man has sown here on earth he will reap in the next world (Galatians 6:7). And there nothing can be added to or subtracted from what we have sown.

The harvest will correspond exactly to the seed that was sown here on earth. God says that He will not be mocked. Whoever sowed 'to the flesh' here on earth – that is, whoever lived in his ego, following the natural impulses of his body, soul and spirit – will accordingly reap destruction. For all that was of the flesh will pass away and fall under the judgment of God. Only that which was sown 'to the spirit' – in other words, that which grew out of a life with Jesus, out of dying to self – produces divine life, joy and glory. When our old man is crucified with Christ, the new man arises, who serves God in truth. And such a person who is filled with divine life will reap bounteous blessings for all eternity.

Let us, therefore, be mindful of the hour of our death when we shall no longer be able to make up for anything. We shall no longer be able to endure in patience, sacrifice or battle on in faith. There will be nothing but a 'seeing' and 'reaping' of that which we have sown in love here amid sacrifices and suffering. This knowledge always helped me in moments when it almost seemed too hard to me to bear the responsibility for an entire Christian organization and go the 'way of faith' in accordance with God's leading for us. Sometimes the yearning would arise in my heart, 'Oh, if only I were in heaven, so that I would no longer have to keep faith!' But then I would say to myself, 'Be grateful that you are not yet in heaven. There you will have no more chances to trust and believe, for everything will be visible to sight. So take advantage of this opportunity on earth. Give thanks that you still have the opportunity to follow dark avenues of faith, which will one day yield an eternal harvest, a crown of faith and the visible outcome of what you believed!'

Indeed, one thought of eternity makes all earthly sorrows fade away. I cannot say how much the thought of death and eternity helped me during days of sorrow. As the waves of affliction threatened to engulf me one day, I began to sing, 'I will rejoice, I will rejoice in suffering here on earth . . . for in heaven I shall no longer be able to suffer.' Yes, more than that -- above we shall rejoice in the same measure that we have patiently suffered here below, for when death comes all values will be reversed.

The Gate of Reality

After our death a gate will open; it could be called 'the gate of reality'. To use an illustration, when in olden days a traveller arrived at the gates of a city, he had to change his money and see how much or little it was worth in the new currency. Likewise at the gate of reality there will be a total reversal of all values, only in a completely different and shattering degree.

The gate of reality, shining with a scintillating brightness, discloses that poverty borne for Jesus' sake means wealth, because the poor are now awarded places in heaven. Disgrace and humiliation in following Jesus now mean exaltation and coronation, for the humbled will be raised to the throne. Those who forwent the love and companionship of others will now have communion with Jesus and all the redeemed in heaven, for 'every one that hath forsaken . . . brethren, or sisters, or father, or mother, or wife, or children . . . for my name's sake, shall receive an hundredfold, and shall inherit everlasting life' (Matthew 19:29 AV).

In this kingdom the sceptre is granted to the long-suffering. They are counted worthy to partake of the glory at the throne of God in so far as they have suffered injustice and insults on earth, for 'if we endure, we shall also reign with him' (2 Timothy 2:12). Now they will taste the blessedness that Jesus promises, 'Blessed are you when men hate you, and when they exclude you and revile you, and cast out your name as evil, on account of the Son of man! Rejoice in that day, and leap for joy, for behold, your reward is great in heaven' (Luke 6:22f). Heavenly laughter will follow the tears that were sown on earth, for as He says, 'Blessed are you that weep now, for you shall laugh.' Those who bore sorrow will now rejoice in the Father's consolation.

Yes, the truth will become manifest at the gate where all

44

values are reversed. But this truth works both ways. It does not apply only to the transformation of sorrow into joy, for Jesus has also showed us what a judgment it can contain for us. He says, 'Judge not, that you be not judged' (Matthew 7:1). Whoever judges and strikes his fellow servants must face the reality of Jesus' words, 'The master . . . will punish him (cut him in pieces), and put him with the hypocrites; there men will weep and gnash their teeth' (Matthew 24:50f). And of the hypocrites Jesus says that they will be sentenced to hell (Matthew 23:33). After the reversal of all values, those who condemned and criticized others and spoke with a sharp tongue will themselves fall under judgment.

Jesus also declares, 'Woe to you that are rich, for you have received your consolation. Woe to you that are full now, for you shall hunger. Woe to you that laugh now, for you shall mourn and weep. Woe to you, when all men speak well of you . . .' (Luke 6:24ff). All this Jesus proclaims as a helpful warning in order to give many more a chance to turn from their old ways while there is still time.

Usually God cannot show us all at once every instance where we have chosen false values and lived according to them. True, the day we gave our lives to Jesus we made a basic change in our set of values by choosing the supreme value, Jesus Christ. And for the first time in our lives we were filled with tremendous joy, for with this changeover of values we had a foretaste of His kingdom, where joy is the predominant feature. Then Jesus continues to open our eyes little by little to the true values, which will bring us the greatest gain for eternity in the hour of death. But if we do not let Him open our eyes, if we do not continue to break with our old values in genuine repentance, we shall backslide and become more and more a prey of the realm of death while we are still alive. The demons, who are then given a right to us by the accuser, will lay hands on us in the hour of our death and keep us in their grip – and the kingdom of glory and joy will remain closed.

How vital it is, therefore, that we learn to reverse our values and change our way of thinking at an early stage! Here on earth we always try to avoid shedding tears and following paths of suffering. We wish to be healthy and to be successful in our careers. We wish to have no family troubles. We wish to have our plans fulfilled and not frustrated. But Jesus states that whoever laughs here, whoever has his fill now – that is, whoever has all that he desires in the way of pleasure, ease and joy – will weep in the next world. A disappointment that cannot be compared with any disappointment on earth! But who takes the matter seriously and realizes that our laughter in the next world will correspond to our weeping here and vice versa?

Satan at any rate is well aware of this truth. And because he begrudges us joy and laughter in the next world, he continually offers us the laughter of sinful pleasure here, for which he will make us pay with eternal weeping, mourning and wailing in his kingdom. At the same time he makes the sufferings of this life, which will bring us immeasurable joy and glory after this brief earthly sojourn, seem unbearably great and detestable, so that we try to avoid them and even rebel against them.

Satan entices us to seek pleasure and satisfaction for body, soul and spirit, instead of being willing to lose our lives as true followers of Jesus. For Satan knows perfectly well that if we are not prepared to give up our rights and our demands for recognition, pleasure, satisfaction and popularity during these short days on earth, we shall suffer great loss in the hour of death. We shall have gained nothing in the way of eternal glory, joy, honour and love – on the contrary, in the sight of the whole world and for all eternity we shall be the ones who are abased and humiliated like Satan himself and all those whom he lured into his kingdom.

Another one of Satan's tactics is to offer us relief whenever suffering enters our lives. He creates diversions and various forms of escapism when we are being chastened. He suggests pills or even drugs for depression, advice from occult sources when we are perplexed and in distress, acts of vengeance when we are hurt, law suits when we are wronged and even suicide when we cannot bear to face guilt and disappointments.

In this way Satan deludes men, making them so foolish as not to think of their death and remember that after a few short years the great reversal will take place. The wise always have eternity and death in mind, knowing that the sufferings of this present time are not worth comparing with the glory that is to be revealed to us (Romans 8:18). The sufferings of this life will soon be over, whereas the sufferings after death will last for ever.

Teresa of Avila, who once had an agonizing visionary experience of hell, later wrote as she recalled the indescribable torments of those brief moments: 'I was terrified by all this, and, though it happened nearly six years ago, I still am as I write: even as I sit here, fear seems to be depriving my body of its natural warmth. I never recall any time when I have been suffering trials or pains and when everything that we can suffer on earth has seemed to me of the slightest importance by comparison with this . . . it has been of the greatest benefit to me, both in taking from me all fear of the tribulations and disappointments of this life and also in strengthening me to suffer them and to give thanks to the Lord, Who, as I now believe, has delivered me from such terrible and never-ending torments.'[1]

[1] *The Complete Works of St. Teresa*, translated and edited by E. Allison Peers (Sheed and Ward, London).

4

A Man Like Any Other?

It stands to reason that the unveiling at 'the gate of reality' signifies that a veil has lain over a person's life on earth. As we can see from Jung-Stilling's *Szenen aus dem Geisterreiche* (Scenes from the Realm of Spirits), evil hides under the cloak of piety. But it also hides under the cloak of diligence, titles and influence, behind fine clothes and a respectable appearance, behind high standards and so-called integrity until the unveiling at death.

But the eternal values of heaven are also often veiled on earth. An example from Holy Scripture is the life of Abraham. He appeared to lead an insignificant life, roaming through the land with his herds like thousands of other nomads. Time and time again he asked God for the son that he had been promised in spite of his advanced age. Years passed by and no son was granted to him. To all outward appearances they were years filled with the ordinariness of everyday life. But that which went on inside him was known to none, except perhaps his wife and his servant. For everyone else he was a man like any other. No one was aware that something tremendous was going on in Abraham's heart – a gigantic struggle with God, an ever new dedication to keep faith and to endure and remain steadfast in temptation, as it is written in the letter to the Romans, 'In hope he believed against hope . . . he did not weaken in faith', even reaching the point where he could believe that God could give life to the dead (Romans 4:17ff).

His faith was underlaid with great suffering. It was a battle of faith. Ever anew he committed himself to continue to wait and to suffer further disappointments from God and nevertheless to wrestle through in prayer until he could trust again. This hidden life of Abraham veiled by a nomadic existence, his suffering, waiting, believing and in the end the sacrifice of that which he had received by faith, had tremendous effects – but not until after his death.

In the moment of death his life was unveiled. It then became evident what his inner life with God was actually like. He was accorded the honour of becoming the father of paradise (Luke 16:22). For over three thousand years now streams of blessing have been flowing from Abraham to his people and all other peoples. By his example millions have been inspired to follow the way of faith. How often I too have been encouraged by the testimony of Abraham's faith in the letter to the Romans! Abraham did not weaken in faith. He believed that God calls into existence the things that do not yet exist and that God sends help and provides a solution when none can be seen. And indeed, God responded to Abraham's hidden and total surrender of himself. 'In thee shall all families of the earth be blessed' (Genesis 12:3 AV) – his seed would be as numerous as the stars in the sky and the dust of the earth (Genesis 13:16; 15:5).

Thus today too future kings, priests and governors (Revelation 1:6; 1 Peter 2:9; Luke 19:19) live in our midst under the veil of obscurity. Their appearance is often piteous. Frequently they receive little recognition and suffer disgrace. But this state of affairs lasts only until they reach the gate of reality. In the meantime the outer covering disguises the true life within them, as the hymn writer Christian Friedrich Richter expressed it:

The life of the Christian glows from within,
Though outwardly they have been scorched by the sun.
The treasures the King of the heavens has giv'n
Are unknown to anyone else but themselves.
What no other soul has e'er sensed or imagined
Adorns their enlightened and radiant souls,
Endows them with majesty, noble, divine.

To outward appearances, oft poor and lowly . . .
Like all sinners they must bear suff'ring and pain . . .
In everyday matters, in sleeping and waking,
Naught seems to distinguish them from other men . . .

But the hymnist is also aware that all values will be reversed,
for he goes on to say:

But when Christ, their Life, is at last manifest
And one day revealed to mankind as He is,
They too will appear with Him, sharing His glory
And reigning victorious as princes of earth.
The whole world, astonished, will see them resplendent,
Adorning the heav'ns as magnificent lights
And then their great joy will to all be revealed.

O Jesus, the Source of the soul's hidden life,
The bright, secret Gem of the innermost heart.
Let us choose obscurity, Thy hidden pathway,
Though disfigured we be by the shame of Thy cross,
Defamed and reviled here, unrecognized, slandered.
We live our lives hidden with Christ in the Father,
But one day exalted with Him before all.[1]

At this I am reminded of our Sister Claudia, who went to
her eternal home at an early age. While she was alive, she
did not seem to stand out among her Sisters, but during her
fatal illness and after her death we could see what tremendous grace blessed her inner life with Jesus. Her great love
for Jesus, which flowed from a heart filled with ever new
contrition, her perseverance in faith inspired by love for
Him and her many acts of dedication then became evident.
Never before had we witnessed how the death of one of our
Sisters brought about a turning point in so many lives as
when the secret of Sister Claudia's inner life was unveiled.
A radiance rested upon her features even as she lay in excru-

---

[1] Christian Friedrich Richter, cf. EKG 265.

ciating pain on her deathbed. And after her death countless numbers were blessed by the little book containing the story of her life.[1]

Thus our hidden life with Christ in God (Colossians 3:3) not only determines our eternal destiny, but continues to be a blessing to those on earth after our death.

[1] Basilea Schlink, *If I Only Love Jesus*.

'Rather fear . . .'

Never are we more afraid than when our lives are in peril.
We would give anything to save ourselves. But now Jesus
tells us, 'Do not fear those who kill the body but cannot kill
the soul; rather fear him who can destroy both soul and
body in hell' (Matthew 10:28). With this all our values are
reversed. Our way of thinking, our sentiments and our attitude towards life are turned upside-down. For almost everyone is afraid of dying. But who – even among believers - is
afraid of being cast into hell, the one thing worth fearing?
In other words, who fears the One who could bring about
such an event – our eternal God and Judge?

The consequences will be terrible if we fail to heed this
admonishment of Jesus. But Jesus does not pronounce these
warnings and threats to make us afraid. When He warns
us, He does so out of love. He does not want us to incur
misfortune, misery and judgment for time and eternity. Thus
whether or not we fear hell and the wrath of God is a decisive
factor for our spiritual life and our eternal destiny. For the
torments and horrors of an existence in hell exceed all human
imagination.

But even the realm of the dead (which is sometimes meant
when the AV uses 'hell') is a dismal place. All the deceased
before Jesus' day came into this realm (*Sheol* in Hebrew or
Hades in Greek), and it was to them that He 'descended
into the lower parts of the earth' (Ephesians 4:9). Likewise
today all those who do not truly accept His redemption or
do not know Him come into this place. Jesus says, 'He that
believeth on the Son hath everlasting life [that is, he will come
into the Kingdom of God, the realm of eternal life]: and he
that believeth not the Son shall not see life; but the wrath
of God abideth on him' (John 3:36 AV). And to be cut off
from life is to be under the power of death.

The fear of the realm of the dead is repeatedly expressed by men of prayer in the Old Testament: 'I shall go down to Sheol . . . mourning' (Genesis 37:35); '. . . to the land of gloom and deep darkness' (Job 10:21); 'For in death there is no remembrance of thee; in Sheol who can give thee praise?' (Psalm 6:5). In the Book of Revelation it is written, 'Blessed are the dead who die in the Lord . . . they may rest from their labours, for their deeds follow them' (Revelation 14:13); but the opposite is true for those who die without knowing Jesus as their Lord and Saviour and for those who even die in enmity towards Him. They will be confronted with a different and terrible reality. When they depart from this life, they take their inner restlessness with them into the next world, and with their restlessness they are even able to have an effect on those who are still alive, as Johann Christoph Blumhardt discovered in his battles with evil spirits. He realized that these accursed souls are also followed by their works – namely, by their sins. It is nothing but unforgiven sin that causes these souls in the realm of the dead such agonizing restlessness and goads them into tormenting others. These observations made by Blumhardt as well as the strict injunction of Holy Scripture not to communicate with the dead (Deuteronomy 18:10ff), which would not have been given if this possibility did not exist, all point to one thing – the deceased in the realm of the dead are not in a state of unconsciousness or sleep, but are fully conscious in this intermediate stage before the Last Judgment. But then the hour will come when Jesus appears in glory 'to judge the living and the dead' (2 Timothy 4:1). Then the kingdom of the dead will open its gates and the dead will come forth for judgment. 'And I saw the dead, great and small, standing before the throne, and books were opened. . . . Death and Hades gave up the dead in them, and all were judged by what they had done' (Revelation 20:12f).

When Jesus refers to the Last Judgment, He says that as the Judge of the world He will condemn those at His left hand with the words, 'Depart from me, you cursed, into the eternal fire prepared for the devil and his angels' (Matthew 25:41). Jesus cannot warn us enough about hell (*Gehenna* in Greek), because it is so terrible. Speaking of it, He says, '[They] will be thrown into the outer darkness; there men will weep and gnash their teeth' (Matthew 8:12; see also Matthew 13:42). Indeed, Jesus considers hell to be so gruesome that He says it would be better for us to maim ourselves and to expose ourselves to the greatest hardships in life in order to experience release from sin and to be saved from the kingdom of hell. 'It is better for you to enter the kingdom of God with one eye than with two eyes to be thrown into hell, where their worm does not die, and the fire is not quenched' (Mark 9:47f). With this challenge Jesus shows us that no torment on earth could even remotely compare with the torment of hell.

When we hear of immeasurable torment – for instance, the torment in concentration camps – most of us probably think that nothing could be more terrible. Yet such places of horror, such prisons and dungeons here on earth are but a very pale shadow of hell, for which Jesus also uses the word 'prison'. None of these sufferings on earth could ever compare with the torments of hell. Nevertheless, the description of the Tullianum, that notorious prison in ancient Rome, helps us to visualize the torments of hell realistically.

This prison, which made every Roman shudder with horror at the mention of its name, was hewn out of a massive rock, the Capitoline Hill in Rome. The Tullianum was a dungeon with no escape. The prisoners were let down by ropes into the murky depths, and high above them at the entrance a strong body of men kept guard day and night. This imprisonment was like being in the antechambers of hell. The prisoners were chained with both legs to an iron ring on the wall, and the rats gnawed at their feet. The appalling stench of rotting flesh – both living and dead – reeked from all corners. Not a single ray of light ever fell into this dungeon. The groans of the prisoners resounded from all sides, but none could see the other, for in these depths – whether it was day or night – darkness reigned permanently.

Teresa of Avila gives a vivid description after her brief visionary experience of suffering in hell:[1]

'I found myself, as I thought, plunged right into hell. I realized that it was the Lord's will that I should see the place which the devils had prepared for me there and which I had merited for my sins. This happened in the briefest space of time, but, even if I were to live for many years, I believe it would be impossible for me to forget it. The entrance, I thought, resembled a very long, narrow passage, like a furnace, very low, dark and closely confined; the ground seemed to be full of water which looked like filthy, evil-smelling mud, and in it were many wicked-looking reptiles. At the end there was a hollow place scooped out of a wall ... and it was here that I found myself in close confinement. But the sight of all this was pleasant by comparison with what I felt there. What I have said is in no way an exaggeration.

'My feelings, I think, could not possibly be exaggerated, nor can anyone understand them. I felt a fire within my soul the nature of which I am utterly incapable of describing. My bodily sufferings were so intolerable that, though in my life I have endured the severest sufferings of this kind – the worst it is possible to endure, the doctors say, such as the shrinking of the nerves during my paralysis and many and divers more ... none of them is of the smallest account by comparison with what I felt then, to say nothing of the knowledge that they would be endless and never-ceasing. And even these are nothing by comparison with the agony of my soul, an oppression, a suffocation and an affliction

[1] *The Complete Works of St. Teresa.*

55

so deeply felt, and accompanied by such hopeless and distressing misery, that I cannot too forcibly describe it. To say that it is as if the soul were continually being torn from the body is very little, for that would mean that one's life was being taken by another; whereas in this case it is the soul itself that is tearing itself to pieces . . . I could not see who was the cause . . . but I felt, I think, as if I were being both burned and dismembered; and I repeat that that interior fire and despair are the worst things of all.

'In that pestilential spot, where I was quite powerless to hope for comfort, it was impossible to sit or lie . . . and those very walls, so terrible to the sight, bore down upon me and completely stifled me. There was no light and everything was in the blackest darkness. I do not understand how this can be, but, although there was no light, it was possible to see everything the sight of which can cause affliction.'

This description gives us an inkling of that which Jesus says about the kingdom of hell: a place of torment, darkness and constant burning, a place where men weep and gnash their teeth. The torment in the Roman dungeon Tullianum came to an end one day for everyone who languished there. But the horrors in the kingdom of hell are immeasurably greater, for there, as Jesus says, 'Their worm does not die, and the fire is not quenched' (Mark 9:48).

To add to the hopelessness of the situation, the soul undergoing torment in the kingdom of hell has barred itself from the realm of the 'Father of mercies and God of all comfort'. The soul is in the domain of the tormentor Satan, who gloats over the misfortune of his subjects and derives the utmost satisfaction from watching their torment as they undergo the dying, burning process. All sadism stems from him. The diabolically-inspired officials of concentration camps mirrored these attributes of Satan and his demons. Often the guards and commanders could scarcely wait for the arrival of a new transport at the camp with thousands of poor victims, whom they would torment to death. Yet how much more are the souls in the kingdom of hell the victims of the tormentor and his vassals, as Jesus warns us in the parable of the unmerciful servant! 'His lord delivered him to the torturers' (Matthew 18:34).

Do we now understand why Jesus bids His disciples, 'Rather fear him who can destroy both soul and body in hell' – that is, fear the holy God? Whoever does not yet have this kind of fear must ask for it. For this command of Jesus is a challenge; it calls for obedience. Jesus' words are not mere words – He will act upon them.

The Second Death and Its Punishments in Hell

To be in the kingdom of hell is to suffer the 'second death' (Revelation 21:8). This means bearing the pain of hell fire for eternity, undergoing fatal burning and destruction without being able to be completely burnt up or destroyed. 'Wherewithal a man sinneth, by the same also shall he be punished' (Wisdom of Solomon 11:16 AV). Likewise in Revelation 16 an angel says, 'Just art thou . . . O Holy One. For men have shed the blood of saints and prophets, and thou hast given them blood to drink' (vv.5f). In other words, the punishments in hell will correspond exactly to the sins committed here on earth. This truth also becomes evident in the story of the rich man, who laments that he must suffer torment in the flames. He felt the agony especially in his tongue, for he asks to have it cooled. Thus the very member with which he had sinned the most was made to suffer the most. God gives each man his due reward.

What horrors will come upon us in the place of punishment if in this life we thought it was too hard to renounce our sinful desires, drives, bitterness, pride, rebelliousness and other sins! Whoever, in this life, did not want to die to self, deny himself and 'lose his life' daily must now die, do without and suffer loss ever anew in a continual process. This was shown, for instance, in a revelation during the first centuries of Christianity and committed to writing.[1]

There was a river of scorching fire in which a number of men and women stood. Some were sunk to their knees, others to their mouth, and others to their hair. Those who were sunk to their knees in this river of fire were religious people who had quarrelled much, especially on their way home from church. Those who were sunk to their lips had

[1] 'Die Paulusapokalypse', *Die apokryphen Evangelien des Neuen Testaments* (edited by H. Daniel-Rops, Zürich, 1956).

slandered each other when they met in church. Those who were sunk to their eyebrows had encouraged each other to cheat their neighbours. One single man was depicted as being completely submerged in this river of fire. His out-stretched hands were bleeding. Worms were crawling out of his mouth and nose. He groaned, he wept and screamed, 'Mercy! I am suffering torment in these pains of hell!' He had formerly been responsible for the administration of the alms, but he had not been honest with the money and had committed fornication – and now he had to suffer these torments perpetually.

The Lord showed other believers that the region of hell for the hot-tempered was a blazing fire of delirium. The spirits there continually mangled each other; they flew at each other with intense hatred; they screamed with horror and yet were unable to let go of each other.

In the region of hell for the immoral, the dead moaned and groaned. Driven by their terrible passions, they per-formed their sodomitical acts, but without deriving any satisfaction from them. On the contrary, their former pleasures have now become an eternal torment for them.

People who no longer wanted to live and hoped to find peace by taking their lives experienced the exact opposite. Unless they were in a condition where they could not be held responsible for their actions, they committed a most serious sin, infringing upon God's right, for He alone is the Lord over life and death. And in the next world they must die continually.

This is confirmed by other reports:

'Just as the murderer returns to the scene of the crime time and again, so does the person that committed suicide. In one village an elderly lady saw a young person leap repeatedly into an outlying lake with suicidal intentions. Investigations revealed that such a suicide had actually taken place there.

'In another case a family with a child was staying at a hotel where the child saw a man shooting himself in their room. Screaming loudly, the child refused to go into the room. Here too a true event was at the root of the matter . . .'[1]

We can understand why Holy Scripture, when speaking of the heavenly kingdom, says, 'While the promise of entering his rest remains, let us fear lest any of you be judged to have failed to reach it' (Hebrews 4:1). Celestial peace surrounds the overcomers in contrast to the turmoil in which the souls in hell find themselves – they are in a constant state of frenzied agitation and continually driven to do their wicked deeds without being able to cease.

The place in hell for the unforgiving was also seen. It was 'filled with a pungent, bitter stench. Figures could be seen there gnawing continually on a piece of wood like a dog chewing a bone, but unable to finish it'. On earth these were people who did not overcome their bitterness. They continually brooded on the same matter and could not get over it. Previously they chose to persist in their bitterness; now they have no choice. A dreadful state of affairs. The troubles that they were unable to get over have now become permanent. 'Bitterness peered out of their eye sockets; the satanic spirits kept throwing them new bones or pieces of wood, so that they always had more to chew – since bitterness, the longer it lasts, the greater it becomes.'

'In the region of hell for the faultfinding, grievances were mounting up. A never-ending trial was taking place; one case succeeded the other. The souls stood in line before the desk of one of Satan's princes, waiting to present their plaint. As soon as their turn was over, they returned to the end of the queue to wait again. There was no end to it.'

Whatever our opinion may be concerning such revela-

---

[1] *Neuer Westeuropäischer Volksmissionsdienst*, Neuss.

tions about the other world, one thing is certain – the second death must be terrible. 'Blessed and holy is he who shares in the first resurrection! Over such the second death has no power' (Revelation 20:6). Do we realize the deep significance of Jesus' words, 'He that overcometh' – that is, whoever has won the victory over sin in the power of His blood – 'shall not be hurt of the second death' (Revelation 2:11 AV)?

'I know that my Redeemer lives!'

Someone has come to take our sins upon Himself! – words are insufficient to express what this means. Only Jesus, the Lamb without blemish, could save us from the punishments of hell, for He alone is sinless. Of His own free will He suffered the infernal horrors of sin and the punishment it incurs, undergoing immeasurable torment. Whoever believes in Him and calls upon His name will experience redemption from slavery to sin and thus will not be under the compulsion to sin in eternity. Only he who bears in mind what hell is realizes what Jesus' atoning death has wrought for us – deliverance from the power of Satan and his claim upon us, salvation from Death and hell.

The way we can thank Jesus the most in this life for His act of redemption is no longer to tolerate sin, for which He suffered such torment, and to fight the battle of faith against it with the utmost resolution.

Yet whoever disregards this tremendous sacrifice of Jesus and continues to sin, despite the fact that our sin inflicted the deepest agony upon Jesus, will incur the most terrible judgment according to the testimony of Holy Scripture. Then the punishment that Jesus bore will fall back upon the person who holds this sacrifice in contempt (Hebrews 6:4–6). And as Jesus was made sin for our sake (2 Corinthians 5:21) and 'bore our sins in his body on the tree' (1 Peter 2:24), so the person who has despised Jesus' sacrificial death will become wholly sin. In other words, all that was dark and evil in his heart will become manifest in his body. The person himself will become the embodiment of hatred, bitterness, rebellion, anger, sensualism, envy, malice and lust for power. This truth was proclaimed by the Prophet Daniel, 'Some [shall awake] to shame and everlasting contempt' (Daniel 12:2). They will bear for ever the curse of sin on their bodies for all to see. Since their natures were characterized by ugly, vulgar features, their outward appearance too can only be repulsive and gruesome in the next world.

But some shall awake 'to everlasting life'. In Christ's kingdom too everything that made up our nature will become manifest and visible. The ransomed ones who live in the City of God are surrounded and permeated by the wonderful light that proceeds from the throne of the Lamb of God, from Jesus, who is Light and Love. He cannot do otherwise than let everyone and everything be bathed in this warm light, for in His kingdom dwell the souls who have been completely pervaded by light. They have endured the all-revealing light here on earth, bringing all that was wicked and evil into the light, however painful it was, and accepted the truth about themselves. Now as the ransomed of the Lord, cleansed of their sins by the blood of Christ, they may walk in His kingdom with bodies pervaded by light. Their hearts are flooded with peace and joy, and as the bride of the Lamb they fill the golden city with their beauty.

'I know that my Redeemer lives!' (Job 19:25) – this they have believed and applied to their lives. The redemption that Jesus wrought shines forth from them and thus they radiate Jesus Himself, the Vanquisher of Death. Jesus, and He alone, could utter those majestic words, 'I am the Life – eternal, immortal life, which Death was unable to touch – and I now grant this eternal, divine life to those who believe.' Indeed, 'he who believes in me, though he die, yet shall he live, and whoever lives and believes in me shall never die' (John 11:25b, 26).

What a gift of grace this hope is in our world of death, for in His resurrection Jesus won the victory over Death, sin and Satan, over all the evil spirits and dominions, whose power is so evident today! In the Word of God a tremendous promise is made to those who love Him – 'If we have been planted together in the likeness of his death, we shall be

5

also in the likeness of his resurrection' (Romans 6:5 AV). We shall be like Him in His resurrection, which contains victory, power, joy and peace. In the light of such a hope Jesus says, 'You will be repaid at the resurrection of the just' (Luke 14:14). Jesus does not want to lead us into the 'resurrection of judgment', which will be the result of evil deeds (John 5:29); rather He wants to lead us into the glorious resurrection life, of which He says, 'Those who have been judged worthy of a place in the other world and of the resurrection from the dead . . . they are not subject to death any longer. They are like angels; they are sons of God, because they share in the resurrection' (Luke 20:35f NEB). If we awake in the Kingdom of God, we shall find everything there imbued with divine life and immersed in joy and ineffable peace.

Do we not all, therefore, have the yearning: 'At all costs I want to partake of His resurrection'? The Apostle Paul shows us the way in the testimony of his life, '. . . that I may know him and the power of his resurrection, and may share his sufferings, becoming like him in his death, that if possible I may attain the resurrection from the dead' (Philippians 3:10f). Thus it is essential to be 'planted together in the likeness of his death'. This means being willing to die to our will, our wishes and desires, yes, to go the way of the cross with Him in order to stand at the side of the risen Lord, the Victor over Death, in the likeness of His resurrection.

HEAVEN AND THE CITY OF GOD –
THE PILGRIM'S GOAL!

Heaven Does Exist

If we wish to describe the essence of all beauty, the most brilliant radiance, the most immaculate purity, we speak of 'heavenly beauty', 'heavenly radiance', 'heavenly purity'. 'Heavenly' means to possess or portray something in perfection. In other words, we are saying that heaven contains the highest measure or fullness of all that is good and beautiful – indeed, its abundance cannot be surpassed. In heaven everything is perfect – in contrast to the imperfection here on earth. This is inevitable, for everything that is connected with God and is under His direct influence reflects His divine nature, which is perfection and abundance.

However, the highest degree of perfection is found in Jesus. He is the essence of all beauty in heaven and on earth. Thus it naturally follows that He fills the heavens with His radiance. In Him we find a concentration of all the splendour of heaven and earth, for He is the 'fairest of the sons of men' (Psalm 45:2) and shines more brightly than all suns.

Light and glory proceed from the countenance of Jesus, flooding the heavens and bathing everything in a wonderful radiance. How could it be otherwise when everything is in direct contact with Him and under His dominion? Nothing can hinder His influence as on earth, where He must first penetrate many layers of sin and break through the forces of evil.

As sure as Jesus is alive and is the greatest reality of all, as everyone who believes in Him has experienced, heaven, the domain of Jesus Christ, is a reality too. And because Jesus is endowed with ineffable beauty and glory, heaven is also endowed with the beauty of God. That is, everything in heaven must be as Jesus is, worthy of Him, befitting Him and reflecting Him.

Jesus has come from this heaven, from the bosom of the

Father, from the realm of eternal joy and glory to bring us to heaven. He has but one desire and that is to save us – to rescue us from Satan's domain and to lead us into His kingdom, where peace and joy reign. In His great love He longs for us to return in joy one day as His ransomed ones to Zion, the heavenly home, where sorrow and sighing shall flee away (Isaiah 35:10).

Sometimes an inexplicable yearning and feeling of joy come over us when we think that there is something other than this dark earth – a kingdom of peace and joy, where there will truly be no pain for body, soul or spirit. Yes, heaven is a reality, and its gates were opened when Jesus was born and the great company of the heavenly host proclaimed the dawning of the kingdom of heaven by singing 'peace on earth'. The heavens were opened over Jesus when He went down into the River Jordan to be baptized for our sake. And ever since Jesus returned home to the heavenly world at His ascension, the gates of heaven have remained open. The cherubim with the flaming sword have departed from the entrance to paradise. This is why Stephen could say when he was accused for Jesus' sake, 'Behold, I see the heavens opened!' (Acts 7:56).

However incomprehensible it may seem, it is an established fact in Scripture that heaven has been open for the ransomed of the Lord ever since Jesus completed His act of atonement. God 'raised us up with him, and made us sit with him in the heavenly places in Christ Jesus' (Ephesians 2:6). This amazing gift of heaven, which has been prepared for us, is an illustration of Jesus' words, 'The Father himself loves you' (John 16:27). Indeed, because the Father in His love wants to see His children happy, He created a heaven where there is nothing but joy and delight. He has prepared His children a wonderful home – not just for a limited period of time, but for all eternity.

In this heavenly home we may taste the Father's love without chastenings. They are no longer necessary, since He has

attained His objective for our lives on earth with the chastenings He sent us. Jesus' victory over sin is fully manifest in all
those who, transfigured into His image, enter their heavenly
home. During their lifetime on earth they battled in faith
against sin, submitting to His chastenings and work of
purification. Now as happy children they rest in the Father's
bosom in the kingdom where there is no sin.

Nor are there any temptations or troubles, sadness or
fear in heaven. Parting and separation, aging and dying,
hunger and thirst, hardships and ordeals are no more. There
man no longer needs to keep faith, for everything is visible
to sight. Heaven is a kingdom where there are no perils to
brave, no loneliness to face, no wants to suffer, no crosses to
bear. There is no one with an evil face, no one in whom
envy, quarrelsomeness or anger still dwells. There are no
tormentors or hate-filled opponents, no persecution, no
slander; for all who have entered the glory of heaven have
become perfect in love – love for God and their fellow men.
In this love for God one and all revolve round the same
centre – our Lord Jesus, the Father and the Holy Spirit,
from whom nothing but love, joy and happiness flow forth.

Heaven means partaking of God Himself, communing
with the Triune God in love, being drawn into His eternal
radiance and peace. And those who are loved by Him and
who love Him in return are granted a foretaste of this here
on earth. They taste the precious comfort His love bestows
upon them. There is a joy that shines like a bright light in the
darkest moments and days of our lives, bringing heaven
down to us when we feel as if we are suffering hell on earth.
Jesus is not far away, He is not only to be found in heaven,
but He comes to His own today and reveals Himself to them.
Indeed, here on earth we can have a foretaste of heaven.

A minister who attended one of our retreats related to us
how he spent nine years as a prisoner of war in the Ural
Mountains under terrible conditions. But, as he testified,
those were the happiest years of his life, for in this immeasur-

able suffering the Lord Jesus drew very near to him. Another minister, who had been in Siberia, told us, 'This hell-like place was heaven to me, because Jesus was present in a way that I have never experienced since.'

If here on earth Jesus' presence can change even hell-like conditions into heaven, by filling us with such joy when He dwells in our hearts, what will it be like when we are really with Him above? After a life of following dark avenues of faith, we shall scarcely be able to grasp it when we find ourselves very close to our Lord Jesus, suddenly hear His voice and behold His countenance, which shines with the radiance of many suns. In the Psalms it is written, 'Thou givest them drink from the river of thy delights' (Psalm 36:8). And what Scripture says is a reality.

This reality of heaven lies behind a legend about a man in the kingdom of the dead. He had spent infinite ages in barren wastes and perpetual gloom, when he suddenly discovered a small opening, not larger than a knothole. When he stood on his toes and craned his neck, he could catch a glimpse of heaven's glory in the distance – a glimpse of the feasts of the blessed righteous. He could hear faint strains of the songs of adoration drifting from the City of God. And so this man stood there on tiptoe, peering and listening with insatiable yearning from one eternity to another – and yet 'between us and you a great chasm has been fixed' (Luke 16:26).

We are still in the body; it is not yet too late for us to give our utmost, so that we do not have to spend all eternity yearning in vain, but may come to 'the city of the living God, the heavenly Jerusalem, and to innumerable angels in festal gathering . . .' (Hebrews 12:22). The way is clearly marked out – it is a matter of pressing on towards the goal of the heavenly calling (Philippians 3:14). And this entails disregarding all earthly values such as personal glory, popularity, power, possessions and human happiness, and adjusting our lives accordingly so as to attain the heavenly prize.

Coming Home!

How wonderful must be the reception in the heavenly world when a soul redeemed by Jesus, a soul for whom He suffered so much, comes home! Holy Scripture says, 'What no eye has seen, nor ear heard, nor the heart of man conceived . . . God has prepared for those who love him' (1 Corinthians 2:9). Above, the Father has prepared something special with which He will receive everyone who has wholeheartedly loved Jesus as his Saviour. This we may count on in faith. Indeed, our hearts should yearn for heaven, since an immeasurable joy awaits us there. What a wonderful entry it will be when the Lord Jesus together with the heavenly hosts receives us in glory!

Since all that is good and beautiful on earth is a reflection of the divine prototype, we can have at least a faint idea of the triumphal reception that a Jesus-loving soul will receive in heaven if he has lived his whole life with the sole desire to bring joy to Jesus, to act according to His word, and to burn himself out for Him in suffering and sacrificing. We think, for instance, of the homecoming of prisoners of war who had languished for years in terrible labour camps. Now they are free and may cross the border again. Once more they hear the familiar sound of their native language. Comfort and joy await them and receptions are prepared for them. Greetings from their hometown reach them at the border and then comes the moment when they are embraced by their loved ones. Home! That which they had pictured to themselves hundreds of times in the faraway country and which had given them hope and strength to endure has now come true. They can scarcely believe it. Their families, inspired by genuine love, simply cannot do enough. They not only gladly fulfil every wish of the homecomer, but they shower him with gifts and make the most marvellous plans for him and his heart almost bursts for sheer joy. But this is merely an earthly experience! What then will it be like when we arrive in heaven where God will so overwhelm us with His love that we shall only be able to stand in awe and worship Him!

Of August Hermann Francke[1] it is reported that in his dying hour he and his family heard wonderful music coming from the next world. Other men of God, as they lay on their deathbeds, saw Jesus or beautiful shining figures coming for them, and they were overwhelmed by the glory of God. One of them even called out, 'O Lord, stay Thy hand; it is enough – more I cannot bear. Thy servant is but an earthly vessel!' If here on earth we feel as though our hearts will burst with joy when Jesus reveals Himself to us, what will it be like when a soul goes home to Him and may behold Him face to face? Then it will be as the Lord said of the ransomed when He spoke through His prophet, 'They shall fear and tremble because of all the good and all the prosperity I provide' (Jeremiah 33:9). Indeed, we shall simply not be able to fathom all that the Father in His love has prepared for us.

All the heavens will be astir when a soul comes home that Jesus was able to prepare as His bride. 'These are they who have come out of the great tribulation' – 'they loved not their lives even unto death' – they fought with the devil and 'conquered him by the blood of the Lamb and by the word of their testimony'. When the gates are opened, the soul will be welcomed by the melodious strains of harps, and holy angels will stand ready to help him join the heavenly hosts in their adoration. And he will be lovingly greeted by the angels and the blessed righteous, who are already in heaven and awaiting him. But what a moment it will be when the ransomed soul has the privilege of beholding face to face the One whom he loves above all else – Jesus!

[1] August Hermann Francke (1663–1727), clergyman and educator in the age of Pietism, founder of the *Franckesche Stiftungen* (schools and orphanages), Halle.

And how wonderful it will be to be led to the Father and to see how He hastens to His child, opening His arms wide to receive him! The Father, who has been waiting for His child to come home, now wipes away every tear (Revelation 7:17). He shows him kindness, comforts and restores him and gladdens his heart. The homecoming child, as it is written, will be clad in white garments (Revelation 3:5) and conducted to his dwelling-place. He is privileged to be at the throne of God for ever. Never again will the child that has come home be able to fall out of this state of grace. The ransomed soul is crowned with everlasting joy, and joy clings to the soles of his feet wherever he goes. Each time he gazes into the countenance of God, he is filled with even greater joy, in so far as this is at all possible.

We shall only be able to comprehend the ineffable glory of heaven if we have fathomed the depths of the love of God – love that since the beginning of time has had nothing but plans for showering His children with all good things. And when we enter heaven, we shall be utterly overwhelmed by this love of His. We shall praise and thank God most of all for having had patience with us, for having sent us chastenings time and again and for not having overlooked any of our sins. Humanly speaking, we would reproach God if He had not been firm with us and we had failed to attain the supreme goal of heaven's glory. Since only those who have been purged of their sinful nature can see this glory, let us give thanks for all the pain and suffering along paths of preparation, which will end in a joyous homecoming in heaven one day.

Now finally dawning
The day of rejoicing,
Of union and love of God and mankind.
O hour full of blessing,
Proclaiming the tidings
That God in His love has brought sinners back home!

Rejoicing and singing,
Sweet melodies ringing
Through all of the spheres of heaven above.
Glad choirs their song raising,
The Lamb of God praising,
And heaven is filled with their rapture and joy.

With anthems resounding,
The Godhead surrounding,
Those ransomed by love now honour the Lamb,
Exulting in worship,
In glad adoration –
Their praises upsoaring in love shake God's throne.[1]

---

[1] Other songs about the heavenly glory can be found in the song-books, *O None Can be Loved Like Jesus*, *The King Draws Near* and *Well-spring of Joy* by Basilea Schlink.

Citizenship in Heaven

Who then will have the right to live in the heavenly Jerusalem? Who will be permitted to walk through its golden streets one day? Who will be granted the privilege to dwell in the palaces of Jesus, the King, to sit at table with Him and behold His countenance of ineffable beauty? Surely, it stands to reason that in such a city where the King of kings resides no paupers with shabby, dirty clothes will be able to live, but rather only priestly, kingly figures (Revelation 1:5f).

A true incident serves as a good illustration. In London there were three sisters living together. One of them was far away from Jesus and completely taken up with the interests of this world. One night she returned home late from a dance. The next morning she was considerably distraught. Her sisters questioned her at length and finally she told them that she had had a dream. It had shaken her deeply. And it was so real that she could still see every detail. She found herself in a city of inconceivable beauty – never before had she imagined such beauty possible. Through the streets of the city people moved graciously with a kingly bearing, their faces radiant with joy. And she saw magnificent palaces, not like those on earth, but pervaded with light and brilliance. The streets seemed to be made of pure crystal. They were luminous and strikingly beautiful. She noticed that all the people who walked by were heading for the same goal, but she felt that she had nothing in common with them.

She followed them to a palace that far surpassed all the others in splendour, a sea of light for sheer beauty and exquisite loveliness. People of all nations were entering this palace and when they came out, they were clad in wonderful, dazzling white garments. As she stood there, everyone passing by called to her, 'Come, do come in. Let yourself be purified and made happy. Then you will be given this wonderful garment!' And one of those hastening past took her by the hand and led her into the palace. With graceful movements the regal figures glided into the hall. All joined in the anthems of adoration and moved to the strains of heavenly music, but she sat disgruntled in a corner. One of the figures moved swiftly up to her and said, 'Won't you come and be happy with us?' Whereupon she replied, 'I don't want to sing with you; I don't know the tunes of your songs. I don't want to dance with you; I don't know the steps of your dances.'

Suddenly she saw Someone step forward, who commanded more reverence than the others and excelled all in beauty, being radiant like the sun. All the music and songs were in His honour. In His presence the faces shone brighter still and the music sounded even more glorious. All the singing and rejoicing were meant for Him – the King of kings, Jesus! He drew near to her and she was immersed in the stream of His unending love. Addressing her, He said, 'Why are you sitting apart? Come and be happy with us and join in the anthems of praise.' 'I don't want to. I don't know the tunes,' she retorted defiantly. 'Then why are you here?' came the thundering reply and at these words the earth opened and swallowed her up.

This was her dream. Her sisters sought to explain it to her and said, 'God was speaking with you.' But she hardened her heart and remained adamant, saying, 'I don't want to.' A few days later she was suddenly found dead with a terrible expression on her face. She had fallen prey to hell.

When we stand before the gates of the heavenly world, may we not have to say, 'I can't go in. Everything here is so foreign to me. I don't know these strains of love and adoration for Jesus and the Father. The world I live in is a different one. Other chords are struck in my heart. I am filled with other interests, earthly interests – my self, my reputation, my well-being!'

We are still living in a time of grace. Jesus is still knocking on the door of our hearts and showing us through the Holy Spirit the way of preparation. We still have the chance now to learn the strains of those who truly love Him, the songs of adoration, by letting ourselves be cleansed and delivered from our sinful ego by His blood. By consenting to the Father's chastenings with a 'Yes, Father', we can still be transformed, so that one day we shall have the right to dwell in the wonderful City of God as citizens and attain the goal of supreme joy as the bride of the Lamb.

It is inconceivable that Jesus Himself has prepared for us a home above. He says, 'In my Father's house are many mansions . . . I go to prepare a place for you. And if I go and prepare a place for you, I will come again, and receive you unto myself; that where I am, there ye may be also' (John 14:2f AV).

After returning home to His Father in heaven, Jesus finally found peace from us sinful men, who did nothing but torment Him. Who can comprehend that He should now desire to have us with Him there! Jesus' love for us is so great that He has prepared a place of rest near Him in His Father's kingdom for those who have abandoned their old sinful ways and dedicated their whole life to Him. And this dwelling-place – amazingly enough! – has been prepared by Jesus Himself, who is the very essence of eternal love and beauty. A dwelling-place of celestial brilliance and loveliness. The perfection of everything that we could possibly desire we shall find in our heavenly home.

How infinitely great is the love of Jesus! He personally concerns Himself with the creation of a palace of imperishable material and untold splendour for each one of us who believes in Him and loves Him. And this dwelling-place will be near Him, because He wants to have us where He is – the Sovereign of the whole universe, lofty and majestic and yet in His love mindful of His ransomed ones.

God alone forges the crown of faith, the crown of eternal

life, and gives it to us, but we attain it by faith, patient endurance and love. And it will be similar with our heavenly home. Even though Jesus prepares this dwelling-place for us and even though it is built by the blood of His wounds, we must supply the building material. The decisive factor is whether or not we have stood the test of faith and suffering here on earth. Whoever wishes to be a citizen of heaven will accordingly bear all hardships on earth with his eyes set on the heavenly goal, which he yearns to reach at any cost.

Thus one could say that the first prerequisite for entering heaven is to be resolute. In this spirit let us pray: 'My Lord Jesus, though I am such an unworthy sinner, prepare me, so that I may come to You in Your heavenly kingdom no matter what the cost. Because I love You and the Father so much and because love for You is the melody ringing in my heart, I can scarcely wait until I am with You and the Father. I cannot bear to live anywhere else but with You. I do not want to have citizenship anywhere else than in Your heavenly kingdom.' Whoever is gripped by this fervent desire sings in his heart:

> Open, O heavens, wide,
> That to my Father's side
> My soul may wing her way.
> My heart already lives
> Above where Jesus is.
> O to be wholly with Him!
>
> This earth is not my home,
> I yearn for heav'n alone,
> Where I'll be one with Christ.
> Then no sin, night or grief,
> None of earth's vanity
> Can separate me from Him.

If this flame is blazing in a person's heart, he will take upon himself everything that is necessary in order to become 'fit for heaven' or 'holy' as Scripture says. He will dedicate himself to the cross and hard pathways and submit to chastening, for he knows that only through chastenings can we share His holiness and without holiness no one will see the Lord (Hebrews 12:10, 14).

Firmly believing in the effectiveness of Jesus' blood and the might of God to inspire both the will and the deed, the soul that yearns for heaven presses on towards the goal of his eternal calling, working out his own salvation with fear and trembling (Philippians 2:12f). He flees the darkness and all its works, for only he who is pervaded with light and who permits the truth to shine into his heart and life will attain the supreme goal. This means that he is willing to hear and accept the truth about himself, to admit and confess his sin. He turns from his old sinful ways ever anew in genuine repentance and calls upon Jesus, the mighty Redeemer, to free him from his bonds of sin, for he wants to attain the heavenly goal. Accordingly, he pursues sanctification; he reaches out for the noble mind of Christ, which is the prerequisite for receiving citizenship in heaven.

Even on earth it is a known fact that when a new ruler comes into power and assumes the reins of government, he appoints ministers who are of his mind and spirit. Similarly, only those who are completely imbued with the spirit of Jesus and live accordingly can dwell and rule with Jesus, the King of kings, in His city.

But what kind of spirit is this? When Jesus is revealed to us above in His royal dignity, enthroned in glory and worshipped by all creatures, we behold Him as the Lamb. The spirit of Jesus is the spirit of the patient, self-sacrificing Lamb. For this reason Scripture says, 'Blessed are the meek, for they shall inherit the earth' (Matthew 5:5). Only those who have this spirit of the Lamb, only those who have died to self and thus become a lamb, whose traits are meekness and humility, have the right to dwell above and rule with Jesus as royal priests for a thousand years (Revelation 20:6).

6

If this spirit of the Lamb, the spirit of patient endurance and long-suffering love, lives within us, we shall reflect Jesus' nature. We shall be with Him above and have the privilege of dwelling in His city. However, if this spirit of the Lamb does not live within us, we shall be unable to endure life there, for the City of God is the kingdom of love, of the meek and humble love of the Lamb, which bears all things, endures all things, is not irritable or resentful and never ends, as Paul says in 1 Corinthians 13. In this kingdom only those will dwell whose hearts are filled with this love. Jesus says, 'By this all men will know that you are my disciples, if you have love for one another' (John 13:35). Those who have this love may behold His countenance as His true disciples. They may be with Him for ever and ever; they have been granted citizenship in heaven.

Jerusalem, the City of God

'The golden city glows with light, reflecting God's own splendour . . .' – that we can sing this is truly no matter of course. If we consider who we are, we cannot understand that God has designed and prepared a golden city for such sinners. In His love the Father considers even the best not good enough for us. By no stretch of the imagination could we ever fathom the glories of the City of God and therefore God has given us only brief indications in Holy Scripture – but even these few statements are sufficient to awaken in us a deep longing, which a hymnist puts into words:

> There is a golden city bright,
> Far, far from tears and suffering,
> And he who sees this place of light
> Will ne'er on earth be satisfied;
> He's filled with secret longing.

The City of God is already in existence; it is the 'Jerusalem which is above . . . the mother of us all' (Galatians 4:26 AV), as Paul writes. This is why it is written in Hebrews 12, 'You have come to Mount Zion and to the city of the living God.' The first-born and the sanctified already dwell above in heaven. However, this place of delight will not always remain distant from the earth. Even now the Lord shows us that the City of God will one day descend upon the new earth, making it like heaven (Revelation 21:2f). What is it that has made our earth so cheerless since the Fall of man? Being separated from heaven, being so far away from God. After the Last Judgment the heavenly Jerusalem will descend upon the new, purified earth, and the dwelling of God will be with men.

In Revelation 21 and 22 Holy Scripture speaks of very real things in this innermost part of heaven, the City of God.

There are gates and streets, trees and fruit, although they are of a completely different substance than the things on earth. Set on high as the centre of the new earth, this wonderful heavenly city will cast its rays upon the whole new earth. This new Jerusalem is endowed with a beauty that no human mind could ever conceive. But God in His love has prepared such glory for those who believed in Jesus and followed Him. He has created Jerusalem for our joy and delight. It is a city filled with light and radiance, beauty and joy, such as no eye has ever seen nor ear heard here on earth. How majestic and gracious are the holy angels who dwell there! How radiant and beautiful the sanctified, whose flowing garments shimmer with light! Translucent and golden are the palaces of the City of God and crystal-clear is the river flowing from the throne of God.

In this city nothing that has been built will be destroyed. Disintegration and death are unknown here. Everything is of a permanent nature. This is a city that will stand eternally. These are bodies that will never decay. Here is a world that contains goodness, love, eternal joy and abundance of life, because God is all in all. Those who loved God above all else, who surrendered every area of their lives to Him, who were entirely pervaded by His light and moulded into His image will one day have their home here, since Jesus, who is the centre of heaven, was the centre of their lives on earth. They can dwell nowhere else now but where He resides – at His throne. What joy to be able to partake of such glory! And all this God has prepared for those who out of love for Jesus sacrificed that which they held dear. Having forsaken everything, they may now inherit everything: thrones and crowns, palaces and riches, the communion of love with the Father and the Son and with all the sanctified.

In heaven the meaning of the name 'Jerusalem' is a reality – 'city of peace'. No sound of complaint or anger can be heard within her walls; a wonderful divine peace reigns here. Jesus, the Prince of Peace, is enthroned here and His glory rests upon everything. But in this city of peace only children of peace can dwell, the meek and peacemakers. For here only words of peace and kindness are spoken – this is what gives the city its character. Everyone who has the privilege of living above in this city as a child of peace is called blessed by Jesus even today and will be called blessed one day by God the Father and all mankind.

But even to pay a visit to the golden city is considered a great honour. This privilege is granted to the nations that have been pardoned at the Last Judgment and live on the new earth. These people have but one wish, one longing – to pass through the gates of the City of God, be it only once. We read that the kings of the nations that live upon the new earth will bring their gifts into the City of God where Jesus lives and reigns (Revelation 21:24). What will it be like when they may behold not only the splendour of this city but Jesus Himself! A stream of love and glory will be poured out over those who are privileged to gaze into Jesus' countenance of beauty and majesty. Even here on earth we say and experience the truth of the words, 'Blessed are the people . . . who walk, O Lord, in the light of thy countenance' (Psalm 89:15).

God Himself is the Architect and Builder of the heavenly Jerusalem. Abraham must have known of the secret of this city. He set out without knowing where he was going and sojourned as a stranger, having no fixed abode, 'for he was looking forward to the city with firm foundations, whose architect and builder is God' (Hebrews 11:10 NEB). If then the Creator of the whole universe builds the capital of creation, this City of God, for His chosen ones, who are to dwell at His throne – what a masterpiece of sublime beauty that will be! For this city God the Father has taken the most splendid material, of which even a granule is very precious, since it is imperishable gold.

God wants us to live for ever in a city with golden streets and brightly shining palaces, where everything is lustrous and brilliant, made of translucent gold, and where we are surrounded by golden splendour. Indeed, in heaven even 'nature' – to use the terms of our world – will mirror our Lord Jesus, being immersed in the wonderful brilliance of His love, as though bathed in gold. In the City of God everything – including every single tree and flower – has been created for the sole purpose of absorbing Jesus' radiant beauty and letting it shine forth in many different ways. In every sense of the word it is a 'Jesus-city', a City of God, where everything reflects the divine radiance.

In a wooded area I was once greeted by an unusual sight when I looked out of the window in the morning. For miles the forest stretched across the hills, tinted by a yellowish gold after the first frosty night. The sun was shining, giving the whole landscape a unique, almost ethereal radiance. Later when the sun was no longer shining, I noticed how shrivelled the autumn leaves were. The enchanting beauty was only produced by the sun. This I took to be an analogy for the mystery of the glorious brilliance and splendour of the golden city. All the radiance proceeds from the throne of God and the Lamb, but this is a sun that will never set.

What details are given of this wonderful City of God, her perfect beauty, sublime magnificence and glory? Priceless treasures are disclosed in the biblical descriptions. The city is surrounded by a wall of jasper, a translucent frosted-white stone, and through it the glorious radiance of the city is shed upon the new earth. No play of colours here on earth can compare with the striking effect produced in the city, where the gold of the streets is set off by the lustrous jasper wall. This wall is described as being 144 cubits high (that is, over 200 ft), but, of course, these human measurements can only give us an inkling of its vastness. This description is intended to show that no man can enter this city by human power and exertion, no man can climb over her wall. Only those who enter through the Messianic door, which is Christ, will be able to pass through the gates of this city. The wall is white as snow to symbolize the divine purity that reigns here. Only pure hearts, in other words, hearts that have been purified, will be able to see God. No trace of darkness will be tolerated. Everything is radiant and lustrous, flooded with the light of purity.

The foundation stones of the wall are fashioned out of different kinds of precious stones and upon them the names of the twelve Apostles are written. When the kings of the earth come and bring their treasures, they are greeted by the names of the twelve Apostles of the Lamb. It is said that as 'members of the household of God', the believers are built upon the foundation of the apostles and prophets (Ephesians 2:20). Thus it is conceivable that the names of the overcomers from all parts of the world, the citizens of this city, are written on the other stones. These are everlasting monuments or 'living stones' as the Apostle Peter says (1 Peter 2:5). Conversely, the names of the great and mighty men of this world will be blotted out for all eternity. We shall behold the names of those who followed the Lamb here on earth, who let themselves be remoulded into His image, who walked in love, humility and lowliness. It is an eternal law as a well-known German song expresses it, 'Those whom You would crown with glory and lift above the sun and stars You first will lead through deeps and valleys.'

Each of the four sides of the wall round the City of God measures 1,500 miles. What are we to infer from this? The largest gem in the world is supposed to weigh 74 grams. But the whole length of this wall is fashioned out of precious gems – an indication of the lavish beauty and magnificence to be found in heaven. Not only are the sufferings of this present time not worth comparing with the glory that is to be revealed to us, but all the beauty and splendour of this world is not worth comparing with the glory, beauty and splendour of heaven. Therefore, blessed are those who are privileged to live in the midst of such beauty from eternity to eternity.

The gates in this wall are also of great value. Each gate is made out of a single pearl, an exquisite work of art. Some commentators mention at this point that pearls are symbolic of tears, since they are formed by the oyster in its pain. Consequently, these gates may well signify that only the path of tears leads into the City of God – tears shed in contrition and tears shed in suffering while undergoing preparation. The gates are wide open and an angel will probably be standing above each gate to greet everyone who enters. It is alone the suffering of our Lord Jesus Christ that has opened these gates for us. Yet even though He suffered and died to open them for us all, the gates of pearl will admit only those who here on earth have truly passed through the door that is called 'Jesus', who have become His own possession and followed Him.

Oh, if only we would bear in mind that every time we enter the narrow gate called 'Jesus Christ', leaving behind the things we hold dear and saying YES to our cross, the gates of pearl will open wider and wider to admit us into the City of God and immeasurable joy one day. Thus only those who here on earth act upon Jesus' words, renouncing everything they have and severing all false attachments for Jesus' sake can be His disciples and one day make a royal entry into the City of God above. There in the heavenly Jerusalem they will be overwhelmed by His love.

> Heaven's astir with joy and delight,
> For Jesus sheds His radiance bright
> Upon the City of God.
> Shining in splendour, glorious and fair,
> The golden city is now prepared
> For the Lamb's Marriage Feast.

Jesus, the Lamb of God, the Centre of Heaven

If the last book in the Bible, the Revelation, gives us a glimpse into heaven, there is one image that shines forth time and again. It is the image of the Lamb, who is worshipped by all the hosts of heaven. Before the Lamb of God stands a great multitude, which no man can number, from every nation, tribe and tongue, clothed in white robes. And with a loud voice they cry out, 'Salvation belongs to our God who sits upon the throne, and to the Lamb!' Further on, we read, 'They have washed their robes and made them white in the blood of the Lamb . . . The Lamb in the midst of the throne will be their shepherd, and he will guide them to springs of living water' (taken from Revelation 7:9–17).

Again, the Lamb is shown standing upon Mount Zion and with Him are one hundred and forty-four thousand who bear the name of the Lamb and the Father on their foreheads. 'I heard a sound from heaven like the noise of rushing water and the deep roar of thunder; it was the sound of harpers playing on their harps. There before the throne, and the four living creatures and the elders, they were singing a new song. That song no one could learn except the hundred and forty-four thousand, who alone from the whole world had been ransomed' (Revelation 14:2f NEB).

What is the song that they are singing? Most likely the song of the Lamb (Revelation 5:9; 15:3). The Lamb is the centre of heaven, loved by all who behold Him. For by His wounds they have been redeemed and they have washed their robes in the blood of the Lamb during their earthly life. How great must be their yearning to stand before Him and behold Him, for He has saved them! Where else can they now stand but before the Lamb? Fervent gratitude and love constrain all who are admitted into heaven's glory to hasten to the Lamb and fall down before Him.

The Lamb has wrought the miracle of redemption by His suffering, by His wounds. At the throne they continue to shine on His glorified body (Revelation 5:6). None of the ransomed of the Lord who now enter glory can behold His wounds without breaking out in ever new adoration for the amazing love of Jesus, who, though God, permitted Himself to be afflicted with wounds. What a deep mystery it is to be able to behold Jesus, the Lamb of God who bears the woundmarks, and to be restored at the very sight of Him whom we have pierced!

Who will love the Lamb of God the most and yearn to be very close to Him above? He who wept over his sins a great deal and ever anew claimed the blood of the Lamb over them. Such a soul will be filled with immense gratitude that he could wash his 'filthy clothes' in the blood of the Lamb every day anew and that they became as white as snow. His love for Jesus is deep and fervent and thus he has but one desire: 'O Lamb of God, to You I must hasten. O Lamb of God, I must behold You. For all the years of my life You were my first and foremost Love. You were my Salvation. By the blood of Your wounds I was transformed. How I worship You! Your wounds shine forth in the heavens as the marks of victory!' Indeed, even here on earth such people are filled with deep longing for heaven. In their hearts a song resounds.

> O Lamb on throne eternal,
> What glory You display!
> If I had wings of eagle,
> I'd fly to You today.
> O joy beyond all measure
> To greet my Lord, my Treasure!

And when His ransomed return home, the Lamb of God will recognize them as those who have lived by the power of His redeeming blood. He knows, 'These are My own; they belong to Me!' He will be their Shepherd and lead them to the eternal springs of water. These springs are fed by His love, for the river of the water of life flows from the throne of God and the Lamb (Revelation 22:1). Thus everyone who drinks of these springs will be filled with even more love for Him.

All who stand with the Lamb upon Mount Zion had but one desire during their earthly life – to follow Him wherever He went. The Lamb of God, the centre of heaven, is surrounded by lambs who followed Him on the way of the cross. The name of the Lamb is written upon their foreheads and this indicates that their nature has become like that of the Lamb. Meek as a lamb they loved those who hurt them, who did them injustice, beat and persecuted them.

How lovingly will the Lamb of God gaze upon those who now bear His traits! Jesus will greatly rejoice to find His image in the 'bride of the Lamb' as the fruit of His immeasurable suffering. These are redeemed souls, pure as virgins (Revelation 14:4) – souls that loved Jesus, their Saviour and Bridegroom, with undivided hearts. They loved Him above all else and, constrained by this love, they gave Him everything, sacrificing even the best they had. This is what made them the firstfruits of mankind, in whom Jesus' redemption was made fully manifest. They returned home as overcomers, for 'no lie was found in their lips; they are faultless' (Revelation 14:5 NEB). Jesus' joy will know no bounds when He beholds these firstfruits, who are so dear to Him; they have been ransomed for God and the Lamb; they are endowed with divine glory and are a worthy reward for all His suffering.

The Lamb in the City of God, worshipped and adored by the bridal host, is radiant with ineffable beauty. His wounds are shining as the marks of His victory. In the lives of His firstfruits this victory has been made manifest. And it will spread – probably beginning with the Marriage Feast of the Lamb – to God's creation, which has been waiting for the sons of God to be revealed (Romans 8:19). Then creation – from the trees and flowers to the animals – will also be redeemed and will join in worshipping their Lord. Indeed, the trees will clap their hands for joy at this redemption, as Scripture tells us (Isaiah 55:12).

Redemption – O blessed word! Redemption – at last the deep yearning of the world is stilled! Redemption has been wrought by the Lamb! Later the nations too will worship the Lamb (Revelation 15:4b). Indeed, the whole universe will be filled with rejoicing and adoration, as it is written in Revelation 5:13, 'And I heard every creature in heaven and on earth and under the earth and in the sea, and all therein, saying, "To him who sits upon the throne and to the Lamb be blessing and honour and glory and might for ever and ever!"' At the throne of God there will be singing of indescribable beauty, not only by the redeemed, who have attained perfection as kings and priests, but by all the angelic choirs. Heavenly strains and melodies, such as no human ear has ever heard, will be raised to give the Lamb the honour and praise that are His due. With manifold variations the words will resound throughout the heavens, 'Glory be to the Lamb! The Lamb has brought the eternal plans of God to completion!'

The heavenly choirs will never be able to cease worshipping the Lamb, and the sanctified will be constrained to raise their songs of praise ever anew. Countless numbers of voices will join in, echoing their praise, as it is written, 'Then as I looked I heard the voices of countless angels. These were all round the throne and the living creatures and the elders. Myriads upon myriads there were, thousands upon thousands, and they cried aloud: "Worthy is the Lamb, the Lamb that was slain, to receive all power and wealth, wisdom and might, honour and glory and praise!"' (Revelation 5:11f NEB).

Oh, probably never before have His own waited so eagerly for this hour as today! But how much more must the heart of God be yearning for this hour! Let us not forget that Jesus is degraded and hated, blasphemed and despised by almost the whole world now, and even in His Church, where His own are falling away in droves and forsaking Him. All this Jesus bears today patiently and silently. But when the apostasy reaches its peak and the Antichrist has appeared, the hour will be near when Jesus will take over the kingdoms of this world. Then 'every knee shall bow . . . and every tongue shall confess that Jesus Christ is Lord' (Philippians 2:10f *The Living Bible*). Then no voice will be able to remain silent any longer.

What is the reason for the singing and rejoicing, for the praises sounding from the lips of all? Not the fact that sorrow and weeping have come to an end and that the old has passed away. Rather it is the revelation of the Triune God in His love that fans the adoration ever anew into flames. It is the revelation of the Father who gave His Son for the world, of the Son who offered Himself as the Lamb for the sins of the world, and of the Holy Spirit who glorifies the Father and the Son. Ever anew the redeemed turn their eyes upon God and the Lamb of God, the Bridegroom, whom they may behold as He is. And each time they are enthralled by His beauty and join in the worship of the angelic choirs, so that the hymns resound throughout all the heavenly spheres and probably even down to the regions beneath the earth.

Indeed, the sight of the Lamb, the glory of His entire being, will so captivate the ransomed that their eyes will never leave Him. At the sight of Jesus' countenance they will be restored, for it is endowed with supreme nobility, majesty and ineffable beauty, with humility, meekness and overflowing love. If there were nothing else to see in heaven, His own would be satisfied for the whole span of eternity with beholding the countenance of the one Lord, Jesus Christ! (Psalm 17:15).

> All praise the Lamb of God,
> Bridegroom and glorious Lord,
> Splendid in majesty.

The Church Triumphant sings,
Making all heaven ring
With joyous strains of praise.

Joy bursts from every heart
Praising the Lamb of God
Enthroned in highest heav'n.
Radiant His countenance –
All feast upon His traits
In heav'n for evermore.

Jesus, belovèd Lord,
By all the saints adored –
The fairest Son of man!
Bowing so reverently
Before His majesty,
They humbly worship Him.

The Marriage Feast of the Lamb

Even on earth a wedding is one of the highlights of a person's life. Yet seen against the background of an earthly, sinful and imperfect life, such a wedding celebration gives us but an inkling of the heavenly Marriage Feast which, unmarred by sorrow, sin and discord or any threat of unfaithfulness or death, will be celebrated by Jesus, the King and Bridegroom, with His bride, the host of those who love Him. The nature of the bride has already been revealed to us in the description of the hundred and forty-four thousand standing before the Lamb upon Mount Zion (Revelation 14). The bride of the Lamb is comprised of those who are privileged to partake in the 'first resurrection', and who are therefore called blessed (Revelation 20:5f), and of those who are raptured at the sound of the trumpet when the Bridegroom comes again in the clouds (1 Thessalonians 4:17). These are souls who were ardent in first love, whose lamps were burning and who had prepared themselves for the Marriage Feast (Matthew 25:10).

The bride, in other words, is the body of true believers. All her members, who are gathered from every Christian church and fellowship, from every nation and people, are one, because they live in perfect love for Jesus and all their brothers in Christ. They will all sit at one table – being one body, one flock, one bride – united in love with their Lord and Bridegroom. In this bridal host, which consists purely of loving souls, there is not a trace of envy, discord or bitterness, which could destroy the harmony and joy. Unclouded unity of love, unclouded happiness! Who can describe the glory of the Marriage Feast of the Lamb! (Revelation 19:7ff)

A wedding celebration on earth receives its radiance alone from the love of the bride and the bridegroom for each other.

If this is missing, a dark shadow is cast upon the wedding and joy cannot break through. But love on earth could never compare with the love that will be manifested at the Marriage Feast in heaven. When the sun of Jesus' love begins to rise and emit its rays, the love of human beings for each other will seem like the flame of a small candle in comparison. Whoever is gripped by His love will also be aflame with love. And the fire of love will set all worlds ablaze, for this love has proved itself. The Bridegroom laid down His life for the bride in love and she in return gave Him her life out of love and gratitude and followed Him on paths of self-denial, where her love was ever anew fanned into a blazing flame.

At the Marriage Feast the Lamb is made one with His bridal host in love, and from this union undreamed-of powers are emitted into the universe. The Marriage Feast of the Lamb – love, joy, never-ending celebrations and jubilation! Now the words of Scripture will be fulfilled, 'At your right hand stands the queen in gold of Ophir' (Psalm 45:9). She stands at His side in exquisite loveliness. She is 'all glorious within', that is, in her heart (Psalm 45:13 AV). She bears the traits of her Bridegroom, having been transformed into His image along the path of suffering as she patiently bore affliction. Now she is given the robe of righteousness, 'fine linen, bright and pure' (Revelation 19:8), because she let her soul be purified. Now she receives the crown, whose splendour corresponds to the humiliation and disgrace that she bore in patience, humility and love for the sake of His name (2 Timothy 2:12). She is arrayed with splendid jewels (Isaiah 54:11; Ezekiel 16:11f) as befitting a bride of the King who rules the universe. Now she shines in splendour in the same measure that she followed her Bridegroom on earth along His paths of humility, lowliness, poverty and obedience, the way of the cross.

Looking back on her suffering, she can only say that the sorrows and chastenings on earth are not worth comparing with such glory. They were necessary to prepare her for the supreme goal, whose fulfilment and climax is the Marriage Feast of the Lamb.

What beauty, what nobility the bride of the Lamb must be endowed with! She is wed to the Sovereign of the world, the King of kings. Once a sinner, she is now raised to His side at the royal throne. Together with Him the bride of the Lamb receives homage from all the heavenly hosts, because she is loved by the King and has been so highly exalted by His grace. But the bride knows who paid the price for her happiness and to whom the honour is due. Thus she is constrained, in humble love, to give all the glory to Him who so dearly loved her and redeemed her. She must love Him with all her heart and thank Him ever anew.

But is this not only natural where love reigns? Each seeks to outdo the other in showing love. The King and Bridegroom wishes to honour His bride and serve her at the heavenly feast; and the bride, filled with the deepest fervour of love and reverence for her King, Saviour and Bridegroom, yearns to give Him the glory and delight Him with the most beautiful song of gratitude, love and adoration. All the heavenly hosts are filled with praise at such humility and love of their Lord and rejoice that ransomed sinners are more richly endowed with grace than themselves.

Do we now understand why there is such rejoicing at the throne? Can we now sense why the song of the redeemed sounds so beautiful? It is the song of love, the song of sinners who, redeemed by His blood, are raised to the throne as the bride of Christ. Joy and delight have taken hold of them. They cannot do otherwise than accord the highest praises to Love eternal for having redeemed sinners by His bitter suffering and death and for making them the bride of the King in His Father's kingdom. Small wonder that all heaven is astir with this praising and rejoicing. There will be celestial dances and the heavenly hosts will fall down in homage before Jesus, the Source of all beauty, the Jewel of

7

heaven, the Delight of the Father and the bride, and the Belovèd of all creation.

Never-ending streams of love flow forth from Him who is Love eternal, and His own are given to drink from the river of His delights at this festive celebration. Now there is nothing more in the way of sin or resistance that would prevent the love of Jesus from flowing into the hearts of His own. The redeemed emanate the love that has been given to them. Filled with adoration, the angels behold their beauty and praise Jesus, the Bridegroom, for having transformed sinners into truly blessed souls, who as the bride of the Lamb now bear His image. The heart of the bride in turn is kindled with adoration by the angels' anthems of jubilation and thus canticle upon canticle is raised until the combined choirs of myriads of myriads surround the throne with their strains of adoration, 'Glory be to the Lamb!'

But how great the joy of the Father will be when He beholds the fruit of His Son's suffering – the bride, a host of sinners who have been remoulded into the image of the Son by His bitter death! 'He will rejoice over you with joy . . . He will exult over you with singing' (Zephaniah 3:17 *The Amplified Bible*). Who can comprehend the joy of the Son as He now presents His bride to the Father! Who can conceive the joy of all creation, which has been waiting for the redemption of the firstfruits (Romans 8:19)! Now they are revealed to sight.

The day of redemption for the whole world, for all creation has dawned. Indeed, one and all rejoice in the day which angels longed to see and for which all heaven has prepared. At last it has come after thousands of years of waiting. Thus we read in Revelation 19: 'Then I heard what seemed to be the voice of a great multitude, like the sound of many waters and like the sound of mighty thunderpeals, crying, "Hallelujah! For the Lord our God the Almighty reigns. Let us rejoice and exult and give him the glory, for the marriage of the Lamb has come, and his Bride has made herself ready"' (verses 6 and 7).

In this hour a celebration will begin in all the heavens, such as has never been seen. The sound of gladness will resound in heaven's spheres as never before – the rejoicing of the Bridegroom and His bride at the Marriage Feast, the expression of their love, which puts an end to the world's hatred of Jesus and banishes the powers of death. At this festival of adoration ten thousand times ten thousand will accompany the nuptial train, dancing celestial dances, singing anthems and bestowing heavenly honours. And most likely the cherubim and seraphim, the princes of the angelic hosts, will take the lead. The heavenly throngs will bow and greet one another. They will break out in ever new thanksgiving, rejoicing and loving. Now the Marriage Feast has truly begun. 'Blessed are those who are invited to the marriage supper of the Lamb!' (Revelation 19:9).

Indeed, blessed are those who are called to the communion of love in the City of God, to the Marriage Feast of the Lamb! Whoever lives with the sole aim of participating in the Marriage Feast of the Lamb prepares himself as a bride day by day. In contrition and repentance he will ever anew let himself be cleansed by the blood of the Lamb and he will walk according to His commandments. What a blessed privilege it will be to enter the gates of the City of God and celebrate the Marriage Feast with Jesus in immeasurable joy!

The Crowning of the Overcomers

The climax of the Marriage Feast of the Lamb is the coronation of the bride, the overcomers. Whoever is very close to
Jesus, the King, will receive a crown. Before his death the
Apostle Paul could say, 'I have fought the good fight, I
have finished the race, I have kept the faith. Henceforth
there is laid up for me the crown of righteousness, which the
Lord, the righteous judge, will award to me on that Day,
and not only to me but also to all who have loved his appear-
ing' (2 Timothy 4:7f).

Our Lord Jesus Himself, who was 'crowned with glory
and honour because of the suffering of death' (Hebrews
2:9), yearns that those for whom He suffered so much may
also be crowned one day. 'Hold fast what you have, so that
no one may seize your crown' (Revelation 3:11b). This calls
for a battle, for the crown is awarded only to the victor. It
is possible to be crowned with 'steadfast love and mercy'
(Psalm 103:4) and to receive 'the unfading crown of glory'
(1 Peter 5:4), 'the crown of life' (James 1:12). 'Golden
crowns' adorn the heads of the elders at the throne of God
(Revelation 4:4). Thus there is not only one type of crown in
the heavenly glory. Jesus Himself bears many crowns
(Revelation 19:12); and the overcomers will receive crowns
according to what they suffered – their afflictions will be
symbolically represented for all eternity by the very jewels
and design of the crown.

Are we pressing on to attain the crown? 'I press on toward
the goal for the prize of the upward call of God in Christ
Jesus' (Philippians 3:14), says the Apostle Paul. But pressing
on means leaving things behind, relinquishing them. Are we
willing to give up our lives and all that makes life worth
living for us in order to win this prize?

A certain event said to have taken place centuries ago is a

shattering illustration about the gain or loss of this crown. This story, known as 'the forty martyrs', has been depicted on many icons. An almost identical event took place this century as we learnt from a report that came from a Siberian prison camp. Ten prisoners were condemned to death. They were made to stand in the freezing cold without any clothes – lined up to be shot before the ditch they had been forced to dig. And in those last few moments they were given one more chance to save themselves by recanting their faith. 'You can save your life, go back to your family, be a father to your children again, if . . .' At this, one of the ten leaves the line, snatches his clothes and renounces his faith. And what happens? One of the soldiers commissioned to execute these ten men sees a wonderful crown resting over the place deserted by the man who had fled death. Gripped by the sight, he throws off his clothes and takes the place of the man who had forsaken his crown. With this act he gives his allegiance to the Lord and lays down his life for Him, who had opened his eyes to see that He awards crowns to those who love Him.

'To him that overcometh will I grant to sit with me in my throne' (Revelation 3:21 AV). 'Truly, I say to you, in the new world, when the Son of man shall sit on his glorious throne, you who have followed me will also sit on twelve thrones, judging the twelve tribes of Israel' (Matthew 19:28). A coronation ceremony awaits us above. Do we realize what this means? It will probably be one of the greatest moments in all eternity when Jesus crowns His bride, placing the crown upon her head before the Father, the myriads of angels, the saints and the whole universe. She will be crowned by the King of kings, so that she may be at His side for ever, seated with Him on His throne, as it is written in His Word. This is so tremendous that it far surpasses our imagination. And the bride herself will scarcely be able to comprehend it. In fervent love and gratitude she will ever anew remove her crown and cast it before her

King and Bridegroom as she pays Him homage (Revelation 4:10).

In order to attain this prize, the crown, people have been willing to undergo the greatest suffering. 'The crown lies before me!' When we say this, even the greatest hardships become easy to bear. A joyous goal shines forth – not only for us, but also for Jesus. Nothing gives Him greater pleasure than being able to award crowns to souls for having kept faith, for having loved Him and given Him proofs of their love by self-denial and sacrifice in everyday life. Now they may inherit the crown. When such grace is shown to sinful men as we are, all the hosts of heaven and all the angelic choirs will fall down in adoration before the Lamb of God. For what is it that alone enables a sinful human soul to receive a crown and be enthroned at the side of Jesus in heaven? Only the blood of the Lamb, His sacrifice, His suffering. We can overcome only 'by the blood of the Lamb'.

O that we may overcome! – everything depends upon this. It is the all-decisive factor. For Holy Scripture says, 'He that overcometh shall inherit all things' (Revelation 21:7 AV) – the crown and the throne. The overcomers are souls who loved not their lives, that is, themselves, but loved Jesus. Because they were willing out of love for Jesus to relinquish their claims, give up their wishes and all that made life worth living for them, they were able to overcome. Indeed, they were even willing to suffer and die for Jesus, because He first loved us and walked the path of suffering for our sakes. And everyone is able to overcome, for Jesus' sacrificial death, His act of redemption and the power of His resurrection guarantee us the victory, provided that we fight the battle of faith. In His sacrifice He has perfected all those who believe in Him and keep faith – theirs will be the crown of life.

When an overcomer, a bride of Christ, receives the crown, all of heaven will be present at the festive ceremony – just as the whole world will witness the Last Judgment. And there is another reason why the adoration and joy of the angels of God will be so great. They know what we are like. Our guardian angels, who served us here below (Hebrews 1:14), were witnesses of everything that occurred during our earthly pilgrimage; they saw our falls, our shortcomings and all that is evil in us, such as bitterness, envy and rebelliousness. Now they stand in awe and worship when they see that sinners, after having followed paths of chastening all their lives, are raised by Jesus to His throne and given the right to judge the nations with Him. Then all of heaven will be astounded and break out in adoration, saying, 'Glory be to the Lamb! He has made sinners and fallen creatures like unto God again. Now they are enthroned at the side of Jesus Christ for all eternity!' Those who have come out of the sorrow and misery of sin are now so transformed that they shine like the sun in their Father's kingdom. 'A masterpiece created out of naught; the Lamb's shed blood this wondrous deed hath wrought!' to quote the hymn, *Who Can Compare with the Bride of the Lamb?*[1]

This glorious outcome of Jesus' work of redemption is symbolized by the crown. It is made of pure gold to signify that on earth our faith has been purified like gold and tested in suffering (1 Peter 1:7). Every act of trust, every 'Yes, Father', every dedication to bear the cross, figuratively speaking, adds to the gold from which this crown is forged in heaven. What significance every day, every hour on earth has when we consider the goal, which is the crown!

Bright crowns God awards now to souls who have followed
In love and devotion the Lamb of God.
They cast them before Him and kneel to adore Him
In blissful rejoicing around God's throne.

The ransomed adoring, a thousand times singing,
'To God and the Lamb be glory alone!',
Surround with their praises the Holiest, Purest,
God Father, Son, Spirit, blest Three in One.

[1] Ernst Gottlieb Woltersdorf.

Life at the Throne of God

'The kingdoms of this world are become the kingdoms of our Lord, and of his Christ; and he shall reign for ever and ever' (Revelation 11:15 AV). When the words of this cry of jubilation become a reality one day as the Marriage Feast of the Lamb begins, life at the throne of God will develop in full. But just as this shout begins to resound through the heavens while the battles with the dragon are still being waged on earth, the overcomers in heaven are being given a taste of the glory at the throne.

Indeed, eternal life reigns at the throne of God – a life of holy abundance in contrast to death and its domain. Truly, this life embraces everything. Complete resting in Jesus and greatest activity in ruling the nations with Him (Revelation 2:26f). The honours received by the overcomers and the homage paid to the Lamb. Loud shouts of joy, singing and adoration and the silent devotion of love for Jesus. Citizenship in the beautiful heavenly homeland, the City of God, but at the same time a holy commission with Him in the various spheres of heaven – the New Testament speaks of 'heavens' in the plural, and the Apostle Paul speaks of three major divisions (2 Corinthians 12:2). Celebrations without end at the heavenly meal, at the Marriage Feast of the Lamb, and service in His kingdom. This is what it means to have 'eternal life'. Its riches and variety are beyond compare.

But since this life springs from God, who is Love, it is harmonious and void of contradictions, stress and strain, exertion and weariness. Everlasting life means life that is inexhaustible and never-ending. At the throne of God there reigns joy that never pales, love that never ceases. Here the body will not grow sick and weak, nor become run-down and worn-out. The palaces in the City of God will never fall into ruin. The trees that grow here bear fruit that never spoils – indeed, these trees keep producing new fruit. And just as this City of God can never be destroyed, the divine love in the hearts of the sanctified and the victorious can never be extinguished.

It is impossible to behold God without being pervaded ever anew by mighty streams of love – and this is the chief feature of life at the throne. In beholding Jesus, sinners are privileged to behold God. We shall 'see him as he is' (1 John 3:2), and yet not perish, although His brilliance is like that of a thousand suns; for we have been washed in His blood and transformed into His image.

If the sanctified did not possess immortal souls and bodies, they would die for sheer joy – life at the throne is so over-whelming. The fiery stream of Jesus' love, which is now poured out over them in His kingdom, would normally consume them. The joy, which breaks out with incomparable force, would normally destroy them. But this is the eternal world, where nothing ever perishes; those who live at the throne of God have been imbued with holy, divine life. God said to Moses, 'You cannot see my face; for man shall not see me and live' (Exodus 33:20). The holiness of God, the consuming ardour of His fire, the full force of His glorious power are far too great for a human being in his earthly nature to remain in the presence of God without being consumed. But people who were always willing in this life to let their sins and all that is wrong in the eyes of God be burnt in the holy fire of His judgment are granted the right to dwell at the throne of God.

For all eternity they may now behold the holy Majesty, God the Father, Son and Holy Spirit, resplendent in the radiance of the throne. The living creatures at the throne are all astir, and trembling with awe, they cry, 'Holy, holy, holy is the Lord of hosts!' Every knee is bent and homage is paid to Him who sits upon the throne and to the Lamb. Here the miracle of full redemption is revealed. Sinners, transformed into the image of God, may now be the bride of the King of kings! And even though man remains a created being and God his Creator, a perfect union is formed, as Jesus says, 'As thou, Father, art in me, and I in thee, that they also may be one in us' (John 17:21 AV) – one in the Holy Trinity.

Perhaps one of the most precious things awaiting His own at the throne of God is that they are actually taken into the mystery of the complete union of the three divine Persons – a mystery of which we can have only a faint inkling here on earth. Revelation 4 and 5 describe the throne of God, where God the Father is enthroned in dazzling splendour (Revelation 4:3). Between the throne and the four living creatures stands the Lamb, 'as though it had been slain' (Revelation 5:6) – Jesus, the Son, who was sacrificed for us. The Holy Spirit is present in the seven torches of fire burning before the throne (Revelation 4:5), and in the seven eyes of the Lamb, 'which are the seven spirits of God' (Revelation 5:6).

How wonderful is the unity of love displayed here at the throne by the Triune God, who is perfect Love! Figuratively speaking, love flows like a mighty river from one Person of the Trinity to the other. The three Persons address one another in the most tender love, while the heavens are filled with the thundering resonance of the homage They pay to each other. One of the highest privileges of life at the throne may well be that the bride of the Lamb is permitted to hear some of these divine conversations of the Trinity, to hear the voice of the Father, the Son and the Holy Spirit, as in perfect love They make Their counsels for governing the entire universe.

The Triune God's perfect unity of love was already manifested to us men in the loving decision of the Father, Son and Holy Spirit to redeem us sinful men. This love cost the Father His most precious possession – His only-begotten Son, whom He dearly loved. Likewise, the Son was prepared to make the greatest sacrifice. For the sake of our salvation

He left heaven's glory and came to earth, completing His course with His suffering and death on the cross, where He offered Himself for us through the eternal Spirit (Hebrews 9:14). And the Triune God is not only completely one in love, but completely one in humility. 'The Father . . . has given all judgment to the Son, that all may honour the Son' (John 5:22f). And the Son does 'nothing of his own accord, but only what he sees the Father doing' (John 5:19). The Holy Spirit glorifies the Father and the Son (John 16:14).

The Holy Trinity at the throne – the most glorious revelation of God! The three holy Persons are one in love – suffering, humble love – but also one in executing judgment. In the end times when sin reigns with its corrosive influence, the love of God, which is true love, will not be able to do otherwise than let His anguished wrath descend upon the earth to purge it. Thus this judgment, which will prove to be a blessing, is an expression of love. When judgment is executed, it is not only the wrath of God the Father that is manifested, but also 'the wrath of the Lamb' (Revelation 6:16). Indeed, the Lamb will set out with the saints to go to war against the powers of darkness (Revelation 17:14). The Holy Spirit too shares in this wrath when flashes of lightning and peals of thunder proceed from the throne in judgment (Revelation 4:5).

The Holy Trinity at the throne of God thus depicts the miracle of complete unity in Their very desires and actions, in Their love and suffering for mankind. But more wonderful than all else is that the Holy Trinity is also one in the desire to bring everything to completion. In Acts Peter says of Jesus, 'Heaven must receive [Him] until the time for establishing all that God spoke by the mouth of his holy prophets from of old' (Acts 3:21). The new heaven and the new earth are the plan of the Holy Trinity. Then the life of perfect unity in love at the throne of God will embrace all things. And we are nearing this goal at a rapid pace.

How wonderful it will be when, after thousands of years

of waiting and suffering, God brings His plan of salvation to its highest degree of completion, as it is proclaimed in Holy Scripture!

Behold, the dwelling of God is with men.
He will dwell with them,
and they shall be his people,
and God himself will be with them
and be their God.
And his servants shall worship him;
they shall see his face,
and his name shall be on their foreheads.
And night shall be no more;
they need no light of lamp or sun,
for the Lord God will be their light,
and they shall reign for ever and ever.

Revelation 21:3; 22:3b–5

Eternal Reward

In one of the last verses of the Bible we read, 'I am coming soon, and my reward is with me' (Revelation 22:12 *The Living Bible*). Reward? Are we permitted to speak of such a thing? This concept came into disrepute during the Middle Ages. In those days people tried to count their merits instead of counting their sins in order to bring them to Jesus, to receive His forgiveness and experience the cleansing power of His blood. This was admittedly an error. But whoever knows the Father's heart of love understands what the Word of God says about rewards and realizes that rewarding has nothing to do with 'legalism', nor is it a concept confined to the Old Testament. These words appear in the New Testament and they cannot be overlooked, since they are part of the Gospel's message, the good news of love. It is the love of God that moves Him to forget our sin and constrains Him to dispense rewards, although there is virtually nothing to reward.

Is it not overwhelming that the Father in heaven should dispense rewards at all? If He were to weigh our lives, placing our sins in one scale and in the other scale all that we have done out of love for Him, all that we have sacrificed or suffered for Him, the scale containing our sins would invariably sink down heavily. There would be nothing left to reward, for the sins would outweigh everything else by far.

But the Father's love is so great that when we repent of our sins and bring them into the light, 'He will tread our iniquities under foot,' as it is written, and 'cast all our sins into the depths of the sea' (Micah 7:19). Indeed, He will remember them no more (Isaiah 43:25; Jeremiah 31:34). He has truly 'forgotten' them. Who can compare with God our Father? The Father loves us indeed. For is it not a sign of love when He covers a multitude of sins, forgets all the evil that has ever been committed against Him and that has wounded His heart so deeply that He lamented, 'You have burdened me with your sins, you have wearied me with your iniquities' (Isaiah 43:24)? Now He knows nothing more of this.

But what does He remember? What has He kept in His heart? The smallest expression of our love – even a cup of cold water that we gave Him by giving it to one of His own. What has He not forgotten? It is written that if someone has received a righteous man, he will receive a righteous man's reward (Matthew 10:40–2). If someone has worked in His vineyard as a co-worker of God, he will receive his wages according to his labour (1 Corinthians 3:8). Indeed those who have served the Lord will receive the heavenly inheritance as their reward (Colossians 3:24) and every secret act of kindness will be rewarded openly by the Father (Matthew 6:3f).

What else has the Father not forgotten? Every tear shed in genuine suffering. He has counted them all (Psalm 56:8) and in heaven He will wipe away every tear from the eyes of His children (Revelation 7:17). But above all, if we have suffered even a little in the way of injustice, slander, disgrace, abuse or persecution for His name's sake, He will reward us richly in heaven according to His promise (Luke 6:22f). And Jesus also promises such a tremendous reward to those who love their enemies (Luke 6:35).

Thus we can see that Scripture often speaks of rewards. The Apostle Paul writes, 'Indeed, God deems it just to repay with affliction those who afflict you, and to grant rest with us [your fellow-sufferers] to you who are afflicted, when the Lord Jesus is revealed from heaven . . .' (2 Thessalonians 1:6f). And in Revelation 11:18 it is written that when Jesus comes into power the time will have come for His servants to be rewarded.

The dispensation of rewards will add to the joy of heaven.

How the Father's heart will rejoice when He is able to reward us there! Our Lord Jesus was sent down to earth to give those who mourn a garland for ashes – that is, to repay their sadness by adorning them – to give the oil of gladness for mourning and the garment of praise for a heavy spirit (Isaiah 61:3; Luke 4:21). Who can conceive what the reward will be like that the Lord will give His own in heaven when they come home after great affliction! What will it be like above when He begins to grant the oil of gladness for affliction and the beautiful white garments of glory for a heavy spirit and when He rewards times of contrition and repentance – this probably being the meaning of ashes – and adorns His own, crowning them with crowns of glory when they enter heaven as overcomers!

Indeed, even here on earth when we have sacrificed things for His sake, the Father cannot do otherwise than repay suffering with blessings. In accordance with Jesus' promise His own have experienced ever anew the truth of the words that whoever forsakes house, lands, brothers and sisters will receive a hundredfold – even in this lifetime! How much more then will the Lord's words come true: 'and in the age to come eternal life'! (Mark 10:29f).

In the life of Job we see how the Father recompensed his great affliction by restoring and even increasing his fortunes. What will it be like in heaven where the Father's reward will be not only a hundredfold as on earth but without end and beyond description! The Apostle Paul testifies, 'This slight momentary affliction is preparing for us an eternal weight of glory beyond all comparison' (2 Corinthians 4:17). It will be impossible to measure this glory by human measurements; there will be no end to it. Have we not already seen how the Father crowned Abraham's hard, dark paths of faith and twenty-five long years of waiting, a time fraught with tears and inner conflicts? He richly rewarded him with untold blessing.

In Malachi 3:16 it is written: 'Those who feared and loved

the Lord spoke often of him to each other. And he had a Book of Remembrance drawn up in which he recorded the names of those who feared him and loved to think about him' (*The Living Bible*). The Father keeps this book of remembrance, so that when we arrive in heaven He can show us the harvest of the seeds we have sown and mete out the reward.

What harvest joys await us in heaven! There the promise will be realized, 'He will come back with songs of joy, carrying home his sheaves' (Psalm 126:6 NEB). 'Everlasting joy shall be upon their heads; they shall obtain joy and gladness' (Isaiah 35:10 *The Amplified Bible*). Here on earth a servant of God has made the most of a few talents. And what will he inherit? Whole kingdoms! His Lord will place him over 'five or ten cities' (Luke 19:17ff). If someone suffered disgrace, slander and persecution for Jesus' sake, he will leap for joy in heaven at the reward he receives, just as our Lord Jesus said (Luke 6:23). And those who have endured in patience and suffered injustice on earth will now rule with Him; in other words, they are appointed to the throne of God and will rule with Him over many (2 Timothy 2:12).

Someone else has followed the path of abasement and humiliation, perhaps suffered much at the hands of his fellow men and was exploited by them. And yet he bore them in patience and love, never growing weary. He was treated like a slave, a doormat, like 'the scum of the earth' as the Apostle Paul said of himself (1 Corinthians 4:13 NEB) – and behold, when he arrives above, the Father welcomes him in order to reward him. Now the words of Scripture are fulfilled, 'He raises the poor from the dust, and lifts the needy from the ash heap, to make them sit with princes' (Psalm 113:7f). Yes, such great honour is shown to this soul in heaven!

Or there is the person who has literally been buffeted about by the storms and gales of life and has weathered hardships of all sorts here on earth. But he humbled himself beneath the mighty hand of God and accepted everything in humility as a sinner who needed such chastening; he was willing to let himself be transformed through these chastisements and trusted the Father along every dark path. Now comes the day of rewarding when the promise made for Zion also comes true for such an overcomer, 'Behold, I will set your stones in fair colours – in antimony [to enhance their brilliance] – and lay your foundations with sapphires. And I will make your windows and pinnacles of [sparkling] agates or rubies, and your gates of [shining] carbuncles, and all the walls of your enclosures of precious stones' (Isaiah 54:11f *The Amplified Bible*).

We are reminded of the wonderful garments of the sanctified, which many an artist has painted, having had a glimpse into the heavenly world – robes of exquisite loveliness, flowing gracefully like silk and velvet, embellished with precious stones and ornaments of an imperishable quality. When the sanctified meet each other in heaven, they will probably be able to tell from the jewels the other is wearing what particular suffering he endured on earth. Now the reward of his suffering can be seen on him for ever; he bears it on him wherever he goes. Now it is no longer the suffering but the outcome that is visible. His cross has brought him all this glory and splendour – garments and gems, a brilliant radiance, a crown and a resurrection body.

According to Holy Scripture, in the heavenly Jerusalem, the City of God, there is a 'festal gathering, and . . . assembly of the first-born who are enrolled in heaven' (Hebrews 12:22f). From this we can infer that the celebration of joyous heavenly festivals will also be part of God's reward. No festival on earth could ever compare with these festivals. And if gifts are often presented at earthly celebrations, this can be taken as a dim reflection of the heavenly festivals where the Father grants rewards: festal robes and costly ornaments, the solace of His love, harvest gifts at harvest

8

festivals, crowns during the coronation. But the festival of festivals, the supreme festival, which both embraces and surpasses all other festivals, is the Marriage Feast of the Lamb. All heaven will celebrate it with indescribable joy and delight.

Indeed, the Father in His love cannot do otherwise than give rewards and He does so abundantly because of the abundance of His love. Therefore, the ransomed and the overcomers will be almost beside themselves with joy as they feast to their hearts' content on the abundance of His house (Psalm 36:8). In response they will break out in ever new worship and adoration. All heaven will be filled with songs in praise of the grace of God, which is manifest in this bestowal of rewards.

Living with Our Hearts in Heaven

In so far as we reckon with the reality of the heavenly world, which has been depicted in the preceding chapters in the light of Holy Scripture, we shall long to be there one day. But there is a great difference between acknowledging this reality with the intellect and actually living in this reality. Whoever does not live in the world above while he is on earth cannot suddenly be at home there later. This we can see from the remark of a Negro servant in Africa. When he returned to the farm after an absence of several weeks, he was told that his master had gone to heaven. At that the servant replied, 'Massa no go to heaven. When Massa plan journey, Massa talk about journey. Massa never talk about heaven. Massa no make ready for heaven. Massa not in heaven.' An almost identical story was related to me about a four-year-old child. When the grandmother died, the child was told that she had gone to heaven. 'No,' said the little girl, 'Grandma's not in heaven. Grandma never told me about heaven. She always told me a lot of stories, but she never told me about heaven. She can't be in heaven.'

Both these replies, simple as they are, contain a spiritual truth. How can a person be at home in heaven one day if on earth he did not live in that which is above and prepare himself accordingly? If the heavenly world was quite foreign to him here on earth, he will not be able to have his eternal abode there after death.

Consequently, it is vital that we, like Abraham, be heaven-bound and that our hearts be set on reaching the heavenly city. We are 'citizens of heaven' (Philippians 3:20 NEB), so let us live in heaven even in this life. During the first few years following my conversion I had not yet fully grasped what it meant to live in that which is above. To be sure I was struck by all the wonderful things I read in Revelation

21 and 22, but they were not a vivid reality for me and did not affect my life. Yet ever since the heavenly world drew near to me, my life has been renewed and filled with over-whelming joy and I have learnt to see things more from the perspective of eternity. The joy experienced here on earth need not be a foretaste of heaven's joy. But for those who live in Christ and in that which is above, all the beautiful things they encounter in this life are a foreshadowing and indication of the coming glory. Thus their joy is deepened. And all hardships too take on a completely new significance.

Living in that which is above truly brings about a reversal of all our values. If here on earth we keep the heavenly goal in mind when we have to follow difficult paths and undergo suffering, we may comfort ourselves with the thought, 'I only have to hold out for a limited amount of time. Then all sorrow will be transformed into eternal joy. In com-parison to this eternal joy, all the transient sufferings of this time are insignificant.' If we have to suffer dark hours or years of loneliness, we have the joyous expectation, 'Above in the City of God I shall for ever be able to partake of the sweet fellowship of love with all those who belong to Jesus.' What an atmosphere of love and understanding there will be! What joy! And if someone has to live in poverty on earth without having a proper home, he has the joyful assurance, 'Above I have a home, with which none can compare and which I shall never have to leave – a home that Jesus has prepared for me near the Father if I have followed Him here below' (see John 14:2f).

Whoever places too much importance on this earthly life and all that he must relinquish and forgo lacks something vital. The heavenly world is not a reality for him. Our years on earth are the shortest ones. They cannot be compared with the ages above, where we shall dwell for ever and ever.

This realization, however, does not imply that we no longer have both feet on the ground, but rather that we draw heaven down into our earthly lives, since Jesus is with

114

us. And wherever Jesus is, there is peace, joy and love – all that makes heaven heaven. It is a fact: God's eternity begins here on earth. The eternal, divine life of heaven seeks to enter our world, so that even now we may become children of eternity. The moment our Lord Jesus, the crown of heaven, came to us, He built a bridge between eternity and mankind. Jesus came to earth, so that it would once more be touched by heaven – yes, that men would learn to long for heaven and that they would henceforth live in heaven while on earth.

Children of eternity are filled with an insatiable yearning for heaven. One could say that a bit of eternity, of the heavenly world, dwells within them. And since they have had a foretaste of heaven, their thirst to enter the heavenly glory and eternity in all its fullness grows ever stronger. Consequently, they hold in contempt all that is earthly and transient and that seeks to bind them to this world, all that allures them and that could preoccupy or even depress them. In spirit they have already been transferred to the kingdom of His beloved Son, as Scripture says (Ephesians 2:6; Colossians 1:13).

Because this spark of love for heaven has been kindled in them, the earthly world can no longer captivate them. They have gained complete mastery over it. They have truly experienced that the joy eternity and heaven brought into their lives is more real and lasting than anything on earth, for the earth and whatever we may possess here can quickly pass away. However, the heavenly life and Jesus' love, which is the essence of life in heaven, can never disappoint us.

During a dark moment in my life I experienced how we are given victory over severe suffering when we fix our gaze on the glory above. One of our young Sisters, who had been ill for a long time, was lying on her deathbed. Agonizing weeks lay ahead of her. She was scarcely able to take in anything, because the pain was so great. How hard it was to stand by and see this; the power of suffering seemed almost indomitable! And yet something was greater than the power of suffering and the approaching death. This was the power of heaven. When I left the sickroom, I prayed that the Lord would grant me something that would comfort and cheer my spiritual daughter. Then He gave me a song about heaven. One verse after the other flowed from my pen – I was scarcely able to stop, for the glory of heaven is so great! I went back into the room, sat down at her bedside and sang this new song to her. She listened attentively and began to sing with me in spite of her weakened condition. Her face began to glow, and the night of pain and sorrow was driven away by the dawning of heaven. The reality of heaven had proved to be stronger.

> Where are true bliss and love?
> Nowhere but above!
> Where trees of life are growing
> We'll walk as though we're dreaming!
> Oh, that we were there!
>
> Where we'll behold Christ Jesus
> In heav'nly fields so glorious.
> Oh, that we were there!
>
> Where, bathed in Jesus' radiance,
> We'll feast upon His countenance.
> Oh, that we were there!
>
> Where we on thrones of splendour
> Shàll reign with Christ for ever.
> Oh, that we were there!
>
> Where we'll forget all sickness,
> Eat fruit of life with gladness.
> Oh, that we were there!
>
> Where God in love will comfort
> His own, from sin now ransomed.
> Oh, that we were there!

Where we'll see all the glory
That God has been preparing.
Oh, that we were there!

Where, filled with joy, we'll wander
In streets of gold for ever.
Oh, that we were there!

It is a mystery when heaven comes down and eternity steps into time. Eternity is a treasure that must be sought and well guarded; it is easily lost if we esteem the treasures of this world more highly. Some may say, 'I too have often sung, "Jerusalem, Thou City Fair and High", but I did not experience that this lifted the darkness about me.' But we must realize that only those who desire this treasure above all else and seek it in time, who pursue it and value it, will discover it. This entails regarding all else as immaterial. For if something is very important to us, we strive for it with all our might, gladly relinquishing everything else.

Now is the time to find this treasure. We must obtain it at all costs. Otherwise we shall never be able to endure the hard times that lie ahead when perhaps very soon we may find ourselves under the shadow of persecution and calamity.[1] We must reach the point where this radiant light of heaven, of the City of God, can break into our lives and heaven can become a reality for us now, in this life.

This was Paul Gerhardt's experience. His hymns will be familiar to many of us. His life was marked by many humiliations and he was even dismissed from his position as a clergyman. He underwent the suffering and distress of the Thirty Years' War and lost five of his children. Thus he was acquainted with much darkness and grief. But his hymns, which usually end with the prospect of heaven, testify that rays of light from the world above had entered his life and that the reality of heaven was greater for him than all the suffering.

[1] See Basilea Schlink, *The Eve of Persecution.*

How did this come about? Giving his consent to God, Paul Gerhardt surrendered earthly things, such as his honour, his position, his children. This is why he could sing when he was suffering disgrace, 'Who there the cross hath shared finds here a crown prepared; who there with Christ hath died shall here be glorified' (cf. *The Lutheran Hymnal*, 192). This shows that whenever Paul Gerhardt was confronted with hardships here on earth he would visualize the corresponding blessing in heaven and thus he was willing to sacrifice the things of this world. This made him joyful in every trial and turned all darkness into light. For when we bear humiliations in the knowledge that these few decades on earth and the suffering they hold will pass by quickly and that we shall be adorned with crowns in all eternity, the cross grows insignificant – indeed, we realize that it actually contains a blessing. Every single experience we have here on earth will have its corresponding recompense in the other world – this we can never engrave deeply enough upon our hearts.

Let us, therefore, live in that which is above. Then the wonderful word 'soon' will be ringing in our hearts. Every time difficulties arise or anxiety wells up in us at the thought of the coming times, we can say, 'Soon I shall be home! Soon I shall be walking on golden streets. Soon I shall see Jesus' countenance of ineffable beauty. Soon, very soon I shall join the bridal host in singing anthems of praise!' If we live with our hearts set on the heavenly goal, eternity can break into our lives and we shall no longer be at the mercy of our troubles, sicknesses, disappointments and circumstances or dependent upon other people. We shall be like kings. All these transient things shall not be able to invade the innermost chamber of our heart. On the contrary, we shall experience that the glory of heaven is born out of the sufferings of this life if we humble ourselves willingly beneath the mighty hand of God, which seeks to prepare us for eternal life by means of chastenings.

We are to live with our lives focused on heaven. Jesus came to earth for this very purpose and God shapes our lives accordingly, so that heaven will have more and more room in our hearts. It is Jesus' deep longing that heaven draw closer to us and eternity become a reality for us, for in the same measure will He, the Lord and King of heaven, become a reality for us. Thus Holy Scripture urges us, 'Seek the things that are above, where Christ is' (Colossians 3:1) – and no longer the things that are on earth.

No other age could have made it easier for us to 'live in heaven' and to 'seek that which is above' than the present one, for no other age has so borne the stamp of hell as ours. At a time when Satan has probably sent his last reserves to earth and has exerted his diabolical influence on more or less everything that we see and hear, our only deliverance is to live in that which is above.

It is vital for each one of us that heaven now become a greater reality than this evil world, which is growing more demonic from year to year. So let our watchwords be:

Live in heaven.

Speak of heaven with one another.

Sing of heaven and it will come down.

Sing of heaven when you are least in the mood to do so.

Now we must bear the reality of the City of God within us as a bright light and goal of faith that always sets us on the right track. Very soon we shall be enveloped in such darkness that we shall only be able to come through if the Light of the City of God – Jesus, the victorious Lamb – illumines everything for us. For He, the King of heaven and all that is therein, is mightier than hell. Before Him hell must yield.

Do we pursue the goal of heaven single-mindedly? If we

fail to do so, we can no longer make up for it when Death stands at our doorstep. But if we live in that which is above, our future home, we shall truly experience that this earthly life with its hardships and sufferings will grow insignificant. Indeed, but one thought of heaven makes all earthly suffering fade into the background; for every type of earthly suffering, as the sorely afflicted Apostle Paul says from experience, has an end; it is limited. This is why it can be called 'slight'. Only that which is endless is hard.

What a privilege it is to live with our hearts set on heaven and the glory of eternity! Indeed, whoever loves Jesus will invariably live in heaven now, for this is where Jesus is. If we love Him, we shall desire with all our hearts to be united with Him above for ever where neither sin nor suffering can separate us. Only in heaven can we behold Him from eternity to eternity, and for this reason souls who love Jesus yearn for heaven. In the same measure that we love Jesus and He is the desire of our hearts, shall we long for heaven, have a foretaste of it here on earth and experience its glory one day above.

Therefore, let us love Him, because He first loved us (1 John 4:19). Jesus has promised that with His Father He would make His home in those who love Him (John 14:23). How much more then will He open His heavenly kingdom to them and grant them a dwelling-place at the throne of God! Love for Jesus is the key to heaven and this love is characterized by the desire to give and sacrifice everything to Him in this life. The City of God, called 'the Bride of the Lamb' (Revelation 21:2, 9f), is inhabited by and composed exclusively of souls who love Jesus. If we love Jesus, we have heaven on earth and one day we shall be near Him in the heavenly glory. The love of God and the soul for each other is the mystery of heaven. Therefore, whoever yearns to attain the goal of the throne, let him say, 'In love I surrender my desires and longings; and lovingly bind myself to Your heart alone.' And one day he will belong to the host of bridal souls – the bride of the Lamb – and enter the gates of His city.

> On earth I wait yearning for that great day
> When I can go home to my Father to stay.
> I'll rest in His arms there for ever.
> On earth I wait yearning for that great day
> When I with my Jesus shall live alway,
> United in love with Him ever.
>
> On earth I wait yearning from day to day
> Till I, free from sin and all toil and pain,
> May enter the heavenly city.
> I think about heaven and do not heed
> The suff'ring on earth, for one day 'twill be
> Transformed into glory for ever.